The 500 Hidden Secrets of
HAVANA

INTRODUCTION

This is a guide that takes you off the beaten track to discover the best places to visit in Havana. You will discover the city's intriguing neighborhoods, its unexpected museums and the coffee bars that the locals love the most.

The aim is to take the reader to unexpected places and to encourage him or her not only to discover Havana but also to really experience the city. We urge people not only to look around but also to listen to the music, taste the food, smell the air and to meet the people, check the Cuban part of Museo de Bellas Artes where one can experience art of the highest quality. Go to Finca Vigía to find the spirit of Hemingway, to Mamainé for a delicious breakfast, and to Starbien for the best *masas de cerdo*. Order an excellent *piña colada* on the rooftop terrace of El Cocinero or a latte at El Dandy.

We highly recommend going to one of the marvellous shows at El Salón Rosado de la Tropical, visiting Casa Compay Segundo, strolling past the statue of Cecilia Valdés, and taking a peek inside the house of writer Dulce María Loynaz. And how about enjoying the refreshing sea breeze on the Malecón, while taking in everything that's going on around you? Once you've been in Havana, you'll surely want to come back.

This book wants to be an intimate, personal and now and then surprising guide to the places that the author would recommend to a friend who would want to discover one of the most special cities in the world, the city where she's lost her heart.

HOW TO USE
THIS BOOK?

This book lists 500 things you need to know about Havana in 100 different categories. Most of these are places to visit, with practical information to help you find your way. Others are bits of information that help you get to know the city and its habitants. The aim of this guide is to inspire, not to cover the city from A to Z.

The places listed in the guide are given an address, including a district (for example Habana Vieja or Vedado), and a number. The district and number allow you to find the locations on the maps at the beginning of the book. Look for the map of the corresponding district, and then look for the number. A word of caution however: these maps are not detailed enough to allow you to locate specific locations in the city. A good map can be obtained from the tourist information center or from most good hotels. Or the addresses can be located on a smartphone.

Please also bear in mind that cities change all the time. The chef who hits a high note one day can be uninspiring on the day you happen to visit. The bar considered one of the 5 best places for live music might be empty on the night you visit. This is obviously a highly personal selection. You might not always agree with it. If you want to leave a comment, recommend a bar or reveal your favorite secret place, you can contact the publisher at *info@lusterweb.co*m. Or follow *@500hiddensecrets* on Instagram and leave a comment – you'll also find free tips and the latest news about the series there.

THE AUTHOR

After having obtained a master's degree in history, Belgian Magalie Raman worked in the record industry for a couple of years, and then found herself working in the world she loves most: the world of books. She likes to read while enjoying a cup of coffee, and she loves to discover connections between books and her other passion, namely travelling and exploring new countries.

One of those travels brought Magalie to Havana in 2005. She instantly knew she would always keep returning there. For more than ten years she has been travelling to Havana, several times a year. Leaving the city is becoming harder every time, and arriving feels like coming home more and more.

What Magalie loves most about Havana are its colors and open-mindedness, its contradictions and energy, its people and dynamism, its cuisine and architecture. The city is always bustling and alive, day and night.

Magalie wishes to thank her husband Nelson Garzón Delis for listening and for sleeping with the lights on while writing. Thanks to her stepdaughter Leidys for keeping her company so often, to her brother- and father-in-law Maikel and Hugo Garzón. Also many thanks to Sofie Devos, Najoua Hamri and Renato Mora for their input and checking out some secrets. *Muchísimas gracias* to Sonia and Salvador, Rafaël, Eli, Tanya and Jorge for making her days in Havana through all those years always a real pleasure. Another thank you is to Dettie Luyten for having the patience of a saint, to Tania Van de Vondel for believing in this project, to the photographer, the graphic designer and the translator. And last but not least thanks to her friends Maïté, Olivia, Heidi, Barbara, Miek and Larissa for their enthusiasm and of course to her parents Lydia and Rey.

HAVANA

overview

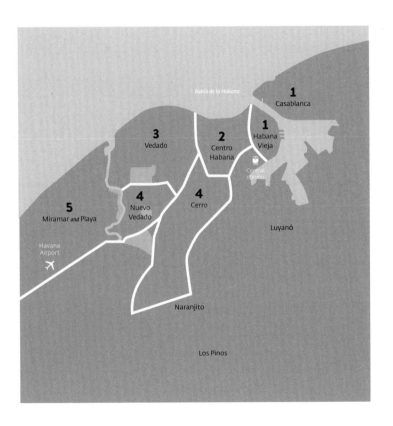

Map 1
HABANA VIEJA

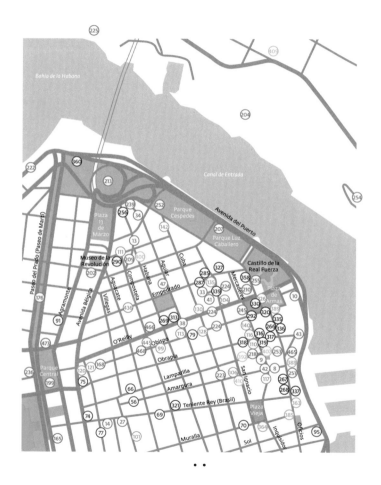

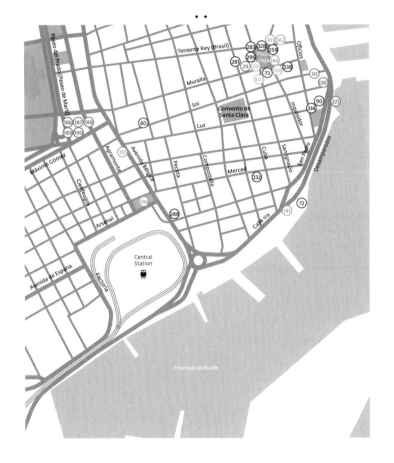

Map 2
CENTRO HABANA

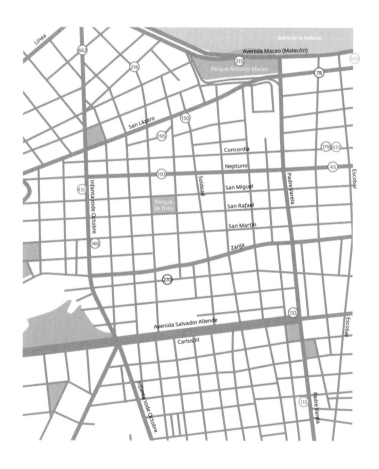

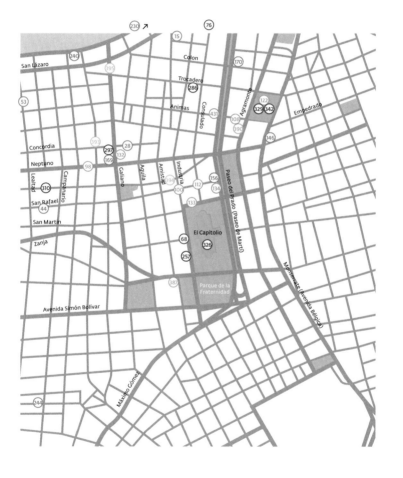

Map 3
VEDADO

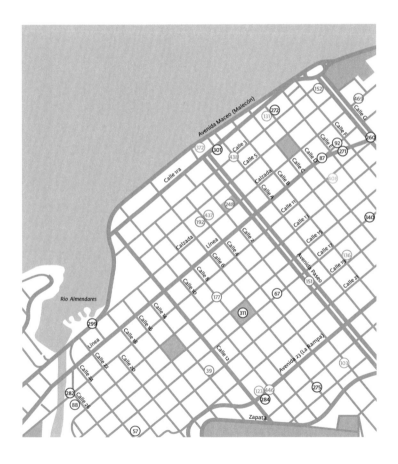

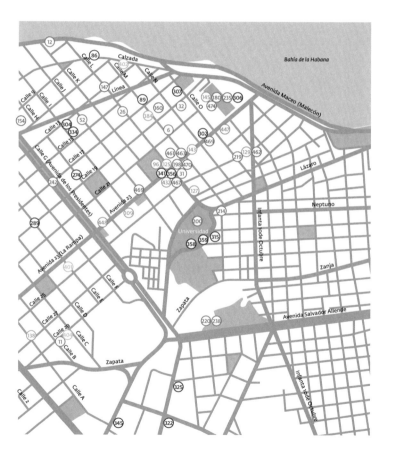

Map 4
NUEVO VEDADO
and CERRO

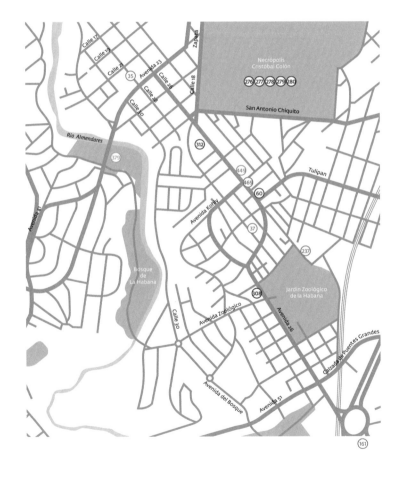

Map 5

MIRAMAR and PLAYA

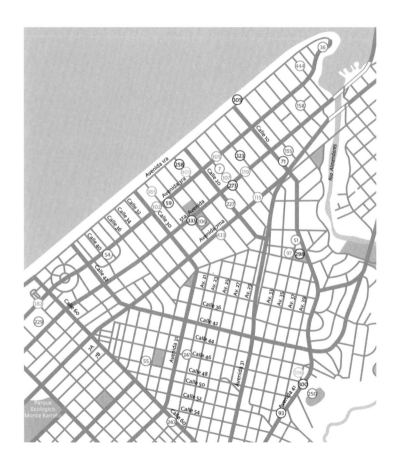

HOW TO READ
ADDRESSES IN HAVANA

Getting oriented in Vedado and Miramar is easy, as the streets are numbered. There are however some peculiarities to take into account. The streets with even numbers are perpendicular to the streets with odd numbers. Also the streets east of Avenida Paseo have letters instead of numbers (letters P to A up to Paseo and there you start counting from 2 up). Every address in this book will look like this: Calle 29 no 205 entre B y C, Vedado. This means that you're looking for street number 29 in the area of Vedado and for house number 205, which you'll find on the block between street B and street C. The word *entre* (or 'e/') will tell you between which streets an address is located. The names of the streets are engraved in the grey stone triangles you'll find on every corner of the street. Sometimes the sign will also say 'esq'; this stands for *esquina*, which means corner. F.e. 'Calle E esq 23' means 'on the corner of street E and street 23'.

In Habana Vieja en Centro Habana streets have names. But here also, the signs will tell you between which streets a certain address is located – and that's very convenient, as the streets here are incredibly long. An example: O'Reilly no 304 entre Habana y Aguiar, Habana Vieja. This means you have to go to the Habana Vieja neighborhood, and look for house number 304 in the O'Reilly street, and that you'll find it on the block between Habana street and Aguiar street. The maps in this book will show you very clearly on which block an address is located. In these neighborhoods you'll find the street name on a sign on the building at the beginning of the street. In Habana Vieja sometimes an old street name will still be in use even though the street now has a new name; you'll probably find both names on the sign (f.e. Calle Teniente Rey is also Calle Brasil).

LA GUARIDA

55 PLACES TO EAT OR BUY GOOD FOOD

---

5 must-try
CUBAN DISHES

---

1 **ROPA VIEJA**

Ropa vieja means old clothes. Immigrants from the Canary Islands brought this culinary tradition to Cuba. There are various myths about this expression. A poor man is said to have cooked his clothes, telling his family that it was good meat and that they would feel less hungry if they believed they were eating good food. According to another myth, a man sold all his clothes to buy food for his family because he did not have enough money to feed them. *Ropa vieja* is a popular dish, a beef stew with vegetables.

2 **POLLO CON QUIMBOBÓ**

A traditional casserole. Chicken is simmered with chopped okra, onions, garlic, green peppers, tomato and plantain, seasoned with black pepper, coriander and lime. This dish is served with a bowl of steamed or boiled malanga and a side of white rice.

3	**TAMALES**	Classic Latin American dish. Prepared by wrapping a mixture of ground corn, masa and other spices in a cornhusk and steaming it. Comes in different flavors and fillings.
4	**CERDO ASADO, MOROS Y CRISTIANOS (CONGRI), PLÁTANO MADURO**	Roast pork in an oven or on a spit. Usually it is served with *moros* and *cristianos*, which accompanies any real comida criolla. *Moros* and *cristianos* is white rice and black beans. Also known as *congrí*. Plátano Maduro is fried plantain.
5	**POTAJE DE FRIJOLES**	Colored or black beans are slow-cooked with garlic, onions, pepper and other herbs to produce this delicious thick soup. Sometimes pieces of pork are added. Served with a bowl of plain white rice.

1 ROPA VIEJA

The 5 best
STATE RESTAURANTS

6 **LA ROCA**
Calle 21 no 102 esq M
Vedado ③
+53 7334501

La Roca lies in the beating heart of Vedado. Here you can eat affordable Cuban food. It is also a great place if you love art deco. At night, you can enjoy stand-up comedy, with comics like Panfilo, a Cuban comic you may remember from the Obama sketch before President Obama's historic visit to Havana in March 2016.

7 **EL TOCORORO**
Calle 18 entre 3ra y 5ta
Miramar ⑤
+53 7204 2209

El Tocororo is Cuba's national bird. The owners created a tropical atmosphere combined with graffiti and fake birds. There is no menu. Your waiter will tell you what are the suggestions. If you want, the cook will prepare what you ask for. Well known for their *mariscos* and *langosta*. Live-music.

8 **JARDIN DEL ORIENTE**
Amargura entre
Oficios y Mercaderes
Habana Vieja ①
+53 7860 6686

The little brother of Café Oriente. Simple dishes with chicken, pork or fish. A relaxed atmosphere in a courtyard with tables around a fountain on a patio with lots of flowers and leafy trees.

9 LA IMPRENTA

Calle Mercaderes no 208
entre Lamparilla
y Amargura
Habana Vieja ⓘ
+53 7864 9581

This is a really nice place. A high-quality renovation of the nineteenth-century imprenta La Habanera. You will be surrounded by letters, old typewriters and printing machines. La Imprenta is open daily from 11 am until 11 pm.

10 EL TEMPLETE

Avenida del Puerto
esq Narciso López
Habana Vieja ⓘ
+53 7866 8807

This restaurant, which has the same name as the Doric El Templete temple, specializes in fish and seafood. You can dine out on the large terrace with splendid views of the bay of Havana and enjoy a pleasant, refreshing breeze. The restaurant's Spanish chef, José Carlos Castillo, pays attention to a pretty and creative presentation of his tasty fish dishes.

9 LA IMPRENTA

The 5 best private restaurants
or PALADARS

---

11 **STARBIEN**
Calle 29 entre B y C
Vedado ③
+53 7830 0711

Starbien stands for excellent food and outstanding service. You can eat inside or outside the Spanish elegant colonial style house. You should try the *masas de cerdo Starbien* and end with a *helado de mamey*. If you prefer fish, choose *pargo en jugo de lima*. Lots of artists, politicians, diplomats and journalists frequent this place.

12 **EL LITORAL**
Malecón 161
entre K y L
Vedado ③
+53 7830 2201
www.ellitoralhabana.com

Another place for great food, with a salad bar with lots of options, which is rather exceptional in Havana. Try the *vaca frita-plátano maduro* followed by *Casquitos de guayaba*. A good time to go is at sunset, while you drink a cocktail and watch the world pass by on the Malecón.

13 **HABANA 61**
Habana no 61
Habana Vieja ①
+53 7861 9433
www.paladarhabana61. com

This tiny restaurant is very close to the Museum of the Revolution and the Santo Angel Custodio Church, on the east side of Havana Vieja. They serve Cuban cuisine with a creative twist. Everything tastes divine.

14 EL CHANCHULLERO

Teniente Rey no 457
entre Bernaza
y El Cristo
Habana Vieja ①
+53 5276 0938
www.el-chanchullero.com

Quite an experience. *"Aqui jamás estuvo Hemingway"*, Hemingway was never here, according to El Chanchullero which is located in a neighborhood where there are a lot of reference to the great writer since it is close to Floridita. Chanchullero means hustler. The devil is in the details so read the menu carefully and you'll soon find yourself laughing out loud with the Chanchullero's modest jokes.

15 LA CALIFORNIA

Crespo no 55
entre San Lázaro
y Refugio
Centro Habana ②
+53 7863 7510

A beautiful nineteenth-century colonial building. The name refers to La California, the neighborhood where the Latin jazz movement started and where people like Chano Pozo, el tambor de Cuba, hung out. Check the illustrations in this paladar. Fresh pasta, pizzas and international cuisine with a creole twist.

11 STARBIEN

5 kinds of
STREET FOOD
you should try

---

16 CHICHARONES

Puffed pork cracklings, sold in paper cones. Buy them from a street vendor, enjoy with a Cristal or Bucanero on a terrace.

17 MANÍ AND CHICHARITAS, MARIQUITAS DE PLÁTANO

Maní are freshly roasted peanuts in paper cones. *Mariquitas* are paper-thin slices of plantain fried in oil. They are sold everywhere. Like *chicharones* this tastes even better with a cold Cuban beer.

18 PAN CON LECHÓN
ROAST PORK SANDWICH

Cubans love their *pan con lechón* or roast pork sandwiches, preferably with crackling. This is the real taste of Cuba. Try one for just 5 pesos moneda nacional opposite the Parque de la Fraternidad. Don't think twice, just go ahead and order one.

19 FRITURAS DE MALANGA

Grated *taro* mixed with eggs and crushed garlic, also deep-fried. A staple on lots of menus. One of the places where you can order them while taking a break is in Plaza San Francisco de Asis, in Hotel Marques de San Felipe.

20 PASTEL DE GUAYABA

Small tarts with a guava filling, sometimes also small triangles of puff pastry filled with guava jam. Either way, they should always be eaten warm. You can buy them on almost every street in Habana Vieja. Another delicious snack to nibble on is *cangrejito de guayaba*, a beignet/donut made on the spot, filled with guava. You can find a vendor in front of the Capitolio, next to sala Kid Chocolate.

The 5 most delicious
CUBAN FRUITS

21 **GUAYABA**

Guava is a tropical fruit cultivated and enjoyed in many tropical and subtropical regions. It is not only consumed as fruit but also used a lot for juices and desserts such as *casquitos de guayaba*, marmalade and pasta. Rich in vitamin C and A.

22 **GUANÁBANA**

Guanábana or soursop is another tropical fruit containing lots of vitamin C, B1 and B2. In Cuba they use it a lot to make juices or smoothies. It's a common fruit drink, you should definitely try it.

23 **FRUTABOMBA**

Frutabomba is the word used in Havana to designate a papaya. You will never hear the word papaya in Cuba's capital, because it also refers to the vagina in Cuban slang. In other cities and regions in Cuba, meanwhile, the word is used for the fruit. If you decide to stay in a casa particular, you will definitely find a large portion of *frutabomba* on your breakfast table, along with some pineapple and a small banana.

24 MAMEY

Whether Cubans refer to fruit, vegetables, meat or fish, they will always make a point of saying how *lindo* (pretty) the food is. I can only agree when they are referring to the mamey, a large, brown, hard fruit, which has beautiful bright orange flesh and a shiny, oblong pit. The mamey is lovely to look at but it is also very tasty, especially in *batido*.

25 MANGO DE BIZCOCHUELO

Most people will already have tasted mangos but there is something to be said for the excellent flavor of Cuban mangos. They come in different colors, sizes and weights, but the sweet *mangos de bizcochuelo* by far are the tastiest ones.

24 MAMEY

The 5 best places to have a
MARVELLOUS BREAKFAST

26 MAMAINÉ
Calle L no 206
entre 15 y 17
Vedado ③
+53 7832 8328

The café was built by the owners themselves. They incorporated recovered elements such as recycled wood, telephone poles and railroad ties in the interior. Enjoy a lovely breakfast on the terrace in front of the café or on the terrace on the side. They also serve cocktails and tapas later in the day. The home-made pineapple and ginger marmalade is divine. Mamainé is a place for art, conversation and friends.

27 EL DANDY
Calle Teniente Rey
no 401 esq Villegas
Habana Vieja ①
www.bareldandy.com

Next to El Chanchullero. A good breakfast place. You can also buy second hand books, original tote bags featuring Kid Chocolate or Hatuey. El Dandy is a personal favourite.

28 CAFÉ ARCÁNGEL
Concordia no 57
entre Galiano y Aguila
Centro Habana ②
+53 5268 5451
www.cafearcangel.com

A coffee bar with 20 types of coffee and vintage style-decoration. The menu is extended to light lunches. Have breakfast here while planning the rest of your day in a pleasant atmosphere while Charlie Chaplin movies are projected on the wall.

29 CAFÉ BOHEMIA

Plaza Vieja,
San Ignacio 364
Habana Vieja ①
www.havanabohemia.com

Decorated with covers of old Bohemias, an old Cuban magazine. Try fresh *jugo de piña con yerbabuena* (pineapple juice with mint) or *Malteado frappé*. The dishes on the menu were inspired by writers, films and journalists. So order an *The Old Man and the Sea*-sandwich or an *El Hombre que Amaba los Perros*, which refers to a book by Leonardo Padura.

30 DULCERÍA BIANCHINI

Sol no 12 entre Oficios
y Avenida del Puerto
Habana Vieja ①
+53 7862 8477
www.dulceria-bianchini.com

If you are a croissant addict and can't live without one for breakfast, then this is the place to go. Their chocolate croissants have taken on legendary status in Havana. Excellent coffee. Quiches, banana bread, ginger cookies, guava biscuits. A second Bianchini opened in Calle San Ignacio no 68.

26 MAMAINÉ

5 places to eat a
QUICK and TASTY
MEAL

---

31 WAOOO SNACK BAR
Calle L no 414
entre 23 y 25
Vedado ③
+53 7830 5264

A fusion of Cuban and Spanish cuisine. Hamburgers, carpaccio and meat with vegetables as well as tapas and cocktails. There are twelve types of gin and tonics. Because who says you always must order a mojito. Two of the waiters were champions in the national cocktail contest. Close to the Museum of Artes Decorativas and Centro Cultural Dulce Maria Loynaz.

32 CALIFORNIA CAFÉ
Calle 19 entre N y O
Vedado ③
+53 5463 0981
*www.californiacafe
habana.com*

Not to be confused with the California Café in Centro Habana. Close to the Malecón which means a nice fresh breeze wafts over the lovely terrace. Mixing the best of California with the best of Cuba. They also serve various vegetarian options such as the Cali-Cuba veggie burger, a meatless *garbanzo* (chickpea)-based burger. Besides the menu, they also have a list of daily specials made with seasonal products.

33 ESTO NO ES UN CAFÉ

Callejón del Chorro,
San Ignacio no 58A
entre O'Reilly
y Empedrado
Habana Vieja ①
+53 7862 5109

Mayrelis Peraza was the curator of the Centro Wifredo Lam for several years. She was inspired by contemporary art when she opened this paladar. She shares her own interpretation of various artworks, combining them with traditional Cuban food and international cuisine. With her cooking she wants to create a delicious tribute to different artists and the visual arts.

34 CAFÉ DE LOS ARTISTAS

Calle Aguiar no 22
entre Peña Pobre
y Avenida de las
Misiones
Habana Vieja ①
+53 7866 2418

Located in what they call *el callejón de los peluqueros* (the street of the hairdressers), where you can visit the hairdresser's museum. This lunch and dining spot serves delicious *ropa vieja* and *tostones* as well as a selection of lighter fish and pasta dishes. The walls are full of photos of Cuban dancing greats.

35 LA PACHANGA

Calle 28 no 254
entre 21 y 23
Vedado ③
+53 7830 2507

Comida rapida or fast food at 3 am in the morning. The owner opened this place with this idea in mind a few years ago. Try the Pachanga burger, a combination of beef, bacon, cheese, egg, olives, vegetables and French fries or the Pollo Pachanga. Also known for their fruit smoothies. Vegetarian options available. A good place to stop after a concert or seeing some art in the Fabrica de Arte. Open till 4 am. A popular spot with *la farandula Habanera*.

The 5 nicest places for a
HEALTHY LUNCH

---

36 RÍO MAR
Avenida 3ra no 11
entre C y final,
la Puntilla
Miramar ⑤
+53 7209 4838

A terrace overlooking the mouth of the Rio Almendares as it flows into the sea. The location is not very eye-catching, but do step inside and you will adore it. The restaurant is close to the sea so do order the tasty swordfish that is served with a layer of guacamole or the grilled fish with octopus or the lobster. The cheesecake with strawberry or guava makes for an excellent dessert.

37 LA CASA
Calle 30 no 865
entre 26 y 41
Nuevo Vedado ④
+53 7881 7000
*www.restaurante
lacasacuba.com*

The Robaina family opened this restaurant in 1995 in their Californian-style house. Their intention was to serve their guests authentic Cuban food according to the recipes of their grandma María Sanchez. Today the Robaina sisters and other family members continue the family's culinary tradition. They have added some new dishes to the menu such as Spanish tapas, Italian pastas and Japanese sushi (on Thursday).

38 O'REILLY 304

O'Reilly no 304
Habana Vieja ①
+53 7863 0206

A trendy and hip spot. The mango daiquiri and the piña colada are to die for. Delicious tacos with a side of black bean paste. Do also try their other restaurant El del Frente, O'Reilly 303. Vegetarian friendly.

39 JUANA LA CUBANA

Calle 19 no 1101 esq 14
Vedado ③
+53 7831 9968

Simple, modest place with outdoor seating at wooden tables. Traditional Cuban food based on organic products. Vegetarian options also available on request. Every second Sunday of the month they invite and focus on local artists.

40 SANTY

Calle 240A no 3023
esq 3raC
Jaimanitas
+53 5286 7039

Located on the western outskirts of Havana. Santy has a wooden outdoor terrace that overlooks the fishing boats. Baby lobster, shrimps, sushi, beef or chicken, everything is excellent here. It's difficult to find and I recommend making a reservation before.

36 RÍO MAR

The 5 best places for
COMIDA CRIOLLA

41 **DOÑA EUTIMIA**
Callejon
del Chorro no 60C
Habana Vieja ⓘ
+53 5281 5883

The owner has developed a very traditional menu based on her memories of her mother's food. She doesn't believe in fusion, all her food is 100% Cuban. *Tamal*, *ropa vieja*, pork, rice and beans. We recommend calling ahead during the tourist season.

42 **LOS MERCADERES**
Mercaderes no 207
entre Lamparilla
y Amargura
Habana Vieja ⓘ
+53 7861 2437

Walk up the staircase, of this magnificent nineteenth-century colonial house, which is scattered with rose petals, to get to this intimate restaurant. The menu features typical Cuban dishes and more international cuisine.

43 **MAMA INÉS**
Obrapía no 60
entre Oficios
y Baratillo
Habana Vieja ⓘ
+53 7862 2669

Chef Erasmo who worked for Fidel Castro opened this paladar in a small street nearby Oficios, which serves Cuban food, mainly pork, with rice, avocado and black beans. The quality of the ingredients is exceptional. Inés does not refer to Chef Erasmo's mother but to a song by Bola de Nieve, called *Ay Mama Inés*.

44 SAN CRISTÓBAL

San Rafael no 469
entre Lealtad
y Campanario
Centro Habana ②
+53 7807 9109

An eclectic decor with references to Cuban culture and heritage. You are transported to the lost worlds that still live on in the work of José Lezama Lima. Maybe you can visit the writer's house before coming here. *Comida criolla con cerdo asado*, *yucca*, *camarones*, *ceviche de berenja o bistec*. Obama ate here in March 2016.

45 ALGARABÍA

Neptuno entre
Gervasio y Escobar
Centro Habana ②
+53 7866 2579

Private cafeteria where you pay with moneda nacional. The best *batido de mamey* in Habana. You can eat on the spot or order take away including the sandwich Cubano (pork, ham and cheese) and the classic *arroz con pollo* (rice with chicken).

41 DOÑA EUTIMIA

The 5 most
AMAZING DESSERTS

46 COPA LOLITA

Copa Lolita. What a delightful name for a delicious dessert. Copa Lolita is made with a bit of flan and one or two scoops of ice cream, usually vanilla or *dulce de leche*. The best Copa Lolitas can be found at Flor de Loto, Calle Salud entre Gervasio y Escobar, Centro Habana.

47 ICE CREAM AT HELAD'ORO

Aguiar 206 entre
Empedrado y Tejadillo
Habana Vieja ③
+53 5305 9131

Look no further for the best ice cream in Havana. Helad'Oro is run by a 'cubanized' French woman and her Cuban husband. Every day they buy fresh fruit from the market, and make the tastiest ice cream with it. Pineapple ice cream unlike any other ice cream you have ever tasted, finger-licking good mamey and guayaba ice cream.

48 FLAN

Flan is the most typical Cuban dessert. You will find it on most menus. Flan is made with eggs, milk, sugar, vanilla and caramel. There are several variants and there's always some space left for a bit of flan after your delicious meal.

49 CREMITA DE LECHE

Cremita de leche is perhaps the most popular streetfood dessert. These hard bars are made of milk and sugar. This tasty sugar bomb is sold by itinerant streetfood vendors but you can also find it at the typical, small market stalls you run into in and outside the city center.

50 CUCURUCHO

Cucurucho is a typical eastern Cuban delicacy, and comes from Baracoa. This mix of coconut, sugar and other ingredients, such as pineapple and guayaba is wrapped in a cone-shaped palm leaf. As this treat is an eastern delicacy, you are less likely to find it here, but keep your eyes peeled and switch on your cucurucho detector.

47 HELAD'ORO

The 5 best places for
FUSION
and other cuisine

---

51 **OTRA MANERA**

Calle 35 no 1810
entre 20 y 41
Playa ⑤
+53 7203 8315
www.otramanera
lahabana.com

'Honest cooking', that is how this enterprising couple promotes their cooking. In 2010, Amy Torralbas, a Habanera, and her Spanish husband Álvaro Diez, who has worked with El Bulli, opened this innovative and contemporary restaurant. The author Wendy Guerra describes this lovely place as follows on her blog 'Habanéame': *"Este no es un restaurant cualquiera, se trata de una pieza vanguardista donde el disfrute es tan importante como la integración cultural de sus recetas. Este es un proyecto colectivo que, siéndolo, no ha perdido su identidad, satisfacción y refinamiento."*

52 **LE CHANSONNIER**

Calle J no 257
entre 13 y 15
Vedado ③
+53 7832 1576
www.lechansonnier
habana.com

Le Chansonnier used to be a French restaurant, which was reopened in 2011 by Hector Figueras. In 2010, the strict paladar act - only a few tables per paladar - was relaxed and has resulted in a culinary renaissance in the past five years. Le Chansonnier is a modern, elegant restaurant with all the cool elements of Havana.

53 CASA MIGLIS

Lealtad no 120
entre Animas
y Lagunas
Centro Habana ②
+53 7864 1486
www.casamiglis.com

Here they combine Swedish and Cuban cuisine. Mr Miglis has been working in the Cuban cinema and audiovisual industry since 1996. He dreamt of establishing this successful restaurant, which he now owns. The beautifully renovated space with high ceilings and a minimalistic interior is the first and for the time being only Swedish restaurant in Havana.

54 LA CARBONCITA

Avenida 3ra no 3804
entre 38 y 40
Miramar ⑤
+53 7203 0261

Can you think of a better place than this green terrace, where you can eat the tastiest pizzas in all of Havana? The Italian chef Walter Ginevri always has suggestions for those who have difficulty choosing. The smiling waiters make everybody feel happy. Definitely call to book a table, especially on Sunday.

55 LA COCINA DE LILLIAM

Calle 48 no 1311
entre 13 y 15
Playa ⑤
+53 5292 5754
www.lacocina
delilliam.com

This family restaurant is inspired by the Brazilian telenovela *Vale todo*, in which Cubans learnt how they could capitalize on an available talent – being a good cook – to open their own business. The enthusiasm was infectious and soon the family received a permit to establish their own restaurant. La Cocina de Lilliam is situated in an elegant home including a garden with fountains. Choose the *lomo especial* or the *tamal de cazuela*.

EL CAFÉ MADRIGAL

40 PLACES
FOR A DRINK

The 5 best places for
COFFEE

---

56 EL CAFÉ
Amargura no 68
entre Villegas
y Aguacate
Habana Vieja ①
+53 7861 3817

Just opened which means, still very much a hidden secret. A good option for breakfast. Exquisite latte and great *cortados* for the morning. Frappes and fresh lemonade for the afternoon. Stop here and you won't regret it. In fact, we bet you will want to come back every day.

57 CUBA LIBRO
Calle 24 esq 19
Vedado ③
+53 7830 5205

A wonderful café with an impressive selection of English books. Cubans and visitors mix and chill on the outdoor terrace. Conner Gorry, a New York-journalist, managed to build a community around good coffee and great literature. The mission of Cuba Libro is to strengthen and support the Havana community in which it operates. A thousand hearts.

58 COSITASS CAFÉ
Avenida 3ra no 2804
entre 28 y 30
Miramar ⑤
+53 5254 0034

Sitting in a *tranquilo* outdoor café among plants in smiling pots while you enjoy a cappuccino or a malta. "Life is good, coffee is better", says the blackboard that also serves as a table.

59 CAFÉ FORTUNA
Avenida 3ra
entre 28 y 26
Miramar ⑤
+53 7203 3376

The taste of coffee in inspiring combinations such as the *Café Miss Ochún* (white rum, banana liqueur, whipped cream and honey), *Café Aroma de Mujer* (Legendario coffee liqueur and ground cinnamon), *Dulce Fortuna* (milk, condensed milk, vanilla and cocoa liqueur and marrasquino) and so on.

60 PICCOLINA
Avenida 26 no 760
entre Avenida Kohly
y 39
Nuevo Vedado ④
+53 7883 0195

This outdoor terrace is just perfect for a coffee break. The place to go for a cappuccino with a banana muffin or a copa Lolita for ice-cream fans. The names of the ice creams refer to the floats at Coppelia. You can order a *Copa Jimagua*, a *Copa Turquino* or *Ensalada de Helado*.

57 CUBA LIBRO

<h1>5 different
TYPES OF COFFEE
for each moment or mood</h1>

---

61 CAFÉ CUBANO OR CAFECITO

Espresso mixed with sugar. Brew espresso, mix some with a small amount of sugar in a metal cup to obtain a paste, add in the rest of the espresso, then pour it all into a cup. The reason why Celia Cruz always yelled *"Azucar"* while performing has to do with the huge amounts of sugar Cubans take in their espresso. One day she asked a café Cubano in Mexico and she received a bitter coffee, which marks the start of her legendary cry for *"Azucar"*.

62 CAFÉ CON LECHE

Coffee and hot milk. Definitely a must in the morning.

63 CORTADITO

Espresso topped with steamed milk. Always sweetened.

64 CAFÉ BOMBÓN

Espresso with a shot of sweetened condensed milk.

65 **CARAJILLO**

A *carajillo* is a café Cubano with a twist. Traditionally a Spanish drink, the *carajillo* combines the café Cubano with rum, brandy or whiskey. In Cuba, rum is the liquor of choice.

61 **CAFÉ CUBANO**

63 **CORTADITO**

64 **CAFÉ BOMBÓN**

The 5 best places for
COCKTAILS *and* TAPAS

---

66 LAMPARILLA TAPAS & CERVEZAS

Lamparilla no 361
entre Aguacate
y Villegas
Habana Vieja ①
+53 5289 5324

This new hot spot is located on a quiet street in Habana Vieja. Every part of this open space is completely decorated with a funky mix of random vintage objects. A big sign reads: "No Wi-Fi, please talk to each other". The tapas menu includes to Cuban, Spanish, Italian and Mexican favourites. The *ropa vieja* is great as well as the pork chops with *zucchini tempura* with a sauce of hot chili.

67 EL CAFÉ MADRIGAL

Calle 17 no 809
entre 2 y 4
Vedado ③
+53 7831 2433
*www.madrigalbarcafe.
wordpress.com*

The Madrigal is more than just a place to eat and have a drink, it is your appointment with Cuban culture. Be surrounded by artworks, photographs and artefacts related to cinema. The owner is Rafael Rosales, a Cuban filmmaker. The name of this very special place, Madrigal, is also the title of one of his feature films.

68 SIÁ KARÁ

Industria no 502
esq Barcelona
Centro Habana ②
+53 7867 4084
www.siakaracafe.com

Contemporary Cuban art, old worn movie posters, old books and Tiffany lamps. It's like stepping into another world. The drinks menu is printed at the back of a licence plate. Choose a deluxe mojito and have some satisfying tapas while conversing with friends. Just behind the Capitolio. Chic Cuban hipsters in an environment with a bohemian vibe.

69 ART PUB

Teniente Rey no 306
entre Aguacate
y Compostela
Habana Vieja ①
+53 7861 5014
www.artpubcuba.com

Not far from Plaza del Cristo and its Chanchullero, you will find this more sophisticated black and white Art Pub. It has an inner courtyard where you can drink terrific cocktails at half price during their happy hour at 6 pm.
Art Pub is a reflection of the new entrepreneurial mindset in Havana. Ariel, the owner, worked as a bar tender at Floridita for many years. He expresses his love of photography in the decoration, with beautiful prints on every wall. The place is littered with old school cameras and photography equipment.

70 LA VITROLA

Muralla no 101
entre San Ignacio
y Cuba
Habana Vieja ①
+53 5285 7111

A small vintage bar with tables inside and outside. There are bicycles suspended in mid-air and old radios on the wall and of course a Vitrola, jukebox. Drink a mojito an order some small plates to share.

The 5 places to enjoy the
COLDEST BEER

71 ESPACIOS

Calle 10 no 513
entre 5ta y 7ma
Miramar ⑤
+53 7202 2921
www.espacios-habana.
com

You feel as if you are entering a 'normal' house but nothing is less true. Once you cross the doorstep, you immediately find yourself in an *espacio* (space) with its own style. These are various spaces, in the same place, which each have their own style and music. The many interiors are resplendent but it is the patio, the back beer garden that I love most, here's the real buzz. Come here late, enjoying the outdoor *espacio* with atmospheric lights and a lot of green. A trendy night oasis to do a lot of talking and drink the coldest Cristals or Bucaneros.

72 CERVECERÍA ANTIGUO ALMACÉN DE LA MADERA Y TABACO

Avenida del Puerto
y San Ignacio
Habana Vieja ①

A microbrewery in an old eighteenth-century tobacco warehouse, near the port of Havana, which overlooks the restored docks. A much appreciated café and restaurant, very popular with the locals. They serve three different types of homemade Austrian beer.

73 **TABERNA DE LA MURALLA**
LA FACTORIA
Plaza Vieja
Muralla esq San Ignacio
Habana Vieja ①
+53 7866 4453

A microbrewery in the center of Old Havana. Light or dark fresh homemade beer on the terrace, patio, underneath the arcades or in the beautifully decorated interior. Drink a *malta* if you don't want to drink alcohol.

74 **KILOMETER ZERO**
no 437
esq Teniente Rey
Habana Vieja ①
+53 7860 0116

A corner with a lot of history. In the twenties there used to be a handbag and belt factory here, called La Imperial. Over time it became the Café Yara, a meeting place for lots of personalities, intellectuals, even armed action groups. Now it's a small black and red bar with photographs of iconic buildings around the capital. If you prefer more privacy, go to the balcony which offers a panoramic view of the bar.

75 **MONSERRATE BAR**
Monserrate y Obrapía
Habana Vieja ①
+53 7860 9761

Order a cold Bucanero or a Cristal for 1 CUC, enjoy a sandwich con bistec de cerdo and listen to some live music. High ceilings and dark wooden panels. Check prices before you order.

75 MONSERRATE BAR

The 5 best places to enjoy a
CUBAN-STYLE COFFEE

**76 CAFETERÍA
   TU PARADA**
   Av. Desamparados
   no 102B
   Centro Habana ②

Coffee is definitely the most popular Cuban drink. In this cafeteria you can order a café Cubano for just 1 CUC, within walking distance of the Malecón. Caffeine and a sea breeze, the perfect combination.

**77 CAFETERÍA
   LA FAMILIA**
   Bernaza no 109
   Habana Vieja ①

Coffee and pizza. That's what the Habaneros buy here throughout the day. Don't be shy, treat yourself to a café Cubano here as a bright start to a new day.

78 BAR MI NIÑA
   San Lázaro no 213
   Centro Habana ②

When the time has come for a sugar-caffeine boost, this is the cafeteria to go for a *cortadito* in the afternoon. A *cortadito* costs two Pesos Cubanos here.

79 CAFETERÍA LA LUZ

Obispo no 157 entre
Aguiar y Cuba
Habana Vieja ①

No matter what time of day, this is the place to go for a caffeine shot. The cafeteria is open 24 hours a day and is always crowded. Order your café Cubano here for one peso moneda nacional. Those small cups of coffee sell out fast.

80 CAFETERÍA SOL Y VILLEGAS

Sol y Villegas
Habana Vieja ①

This is an example of one of the many inventive ways in which Cubans make a living. They sell coffee out of their window. And good coffee too. Try some like the real Habaneros. Kick-start your day with a sweet shot of café Cubano. They also sell Coffee Mate here.

The 5 most exotic
NON-ALCOHOLIC DRINKS

---

81 PRU

Pru is a refreshing brown-colored drink with medicinal properties. It was brought to Cuba by French colonialists after the Haitian Revolution. It was originally produced in the eastern part of the island. Nowadays, however, it is sold all over the country. This is usually a homemade brew. Everything starts with the fermentation of several plant roots, along with chinaberry, Chinese root, pepper leaves, brown sugar, cinnamon, pine sprouts and water. There are people who add their own ingredients to impart a unique flavor to the drink. Once everything is thoroughly blended, the mixture is poured into a container that is carefully sealed so it can ferment. As for its medicinal properties, this anti-oxidant supposedly lowers blood pressure.

82 **GUARAPO**

Sugarcane juice to give you sufficient energy to explore the 500 secrets of Havana. Try this at La Guarapera, Lagunas esq Gervasio, Centro Habana.

83 **LIMONADA FRAPPÉ**

Lemon juice, water and sugar, crushed ice, mint. Lots of vitamin C. Refreshing and promotes good digestion.

84 **BATIDO DE MAMEY, BATIDO DE FRUTABOMBA, BATIDO DE GUAYABA**

You can drink these fruity smoothies in lots of places. Everyone has a different take. Some add ice cream, others milk or condensed milk. Always sweetened, these *batidos* are obviously very addictive. *Frutabomba* is papaya.

85 **JUGO DE PIÑA CON YERBA BUENA**

It may sound like a drink with hallucinatory properties but it is anything but. This pineapple juice, which is blended with mint leaves, is probably one of the most refreshing drinks you'll ever taste. A delicious way to unwind after a busy day. Café Bohemia has the best in Havana.

The 5 most
STUNNING ROOFTOPS

---

86 CAFÉ LA FLAUTA MAGICA
Calzada 101
entre L y M
Vedado ③
+53 7832 3195

Named after Richard Egües, a flute player in Cuba's legendary Orquesta Aragon whose nickname was 'the magic flute'. This bar is located on the top floor of the building opposite the U.S. Embassy. There are no signs of a bar when you get there. Don't be shy, take the elevator to the 10th floor. Enjoy some amazing views of Havana from this fancy rooftop with swimming pool. Order a daiquiri and frituras de Malanga while listening to some smooth live jazz tunes.

87 VERSUS 1900
Línea no 504 entre D y E
Vedado ③
+53 7835 1852

This house was built in… yes, that's right, in 1900. Enjoy a mojito and chill out on this superior terrace. There are beds and sofas.

88 EL COCINERO
Calle 26 entre 11 y 13
Vedado ③
+53 7832 2355

This industrial chic open air rooftop is a true gem and serves the best piña colada. Located underneath the imposing eponymously named brick chimney, this trendy bar should be on your absolutely must do-list. Fantastic tapas and food.

89 BAR LA TORRE
Edificio Focsa,
Calle 17 esq M
Vedado ③
+53 7553088

Bar la Torre is located in the FOCSA building, the highest building in Havana. The FOCSA building is considered one of the seven wonders of Cuban civil engineering. Go to the bar on the 33th floor to see the sunset from the highest point over Havana while sipping a cocktail.

90 TERRAZA HOTEL ARMADORES DE SANTANDER
Luz esq San Pedro
Habana Vieja ①
+53 7862 8000

This great rooftop terrace of Hotel Armadores de Santander has a splendid view of the port and its bay, as well as the Russian church. Although the terrace is close to city's busy historic center, you can enjoy some peace and quiet here, high above the other buildings. It's also a nice breakfast place where you can enjoy the fresh breeze of El Malecón.

89 EL COCINERO

5

TRADITIONAL *versus* CONTEMPORARY BARS

---

91 SLOPPY JOE'S
Animas esq Zulueta
Habana Vieja ①
+53 7866 7157
www.sloppyjoes.org

An immense bar with an even bigger history. The bar reopened in 2013 after being closed for 48 years. Sloppy Joe's was popular with U.S. tourists in the twenties and thirties during the Prohibition, when they made Havana their playground. This bar is also featured in the movie *Our man in Havana*. Try the Sloppy Joe cocktail, a cool refreshing blend of brandy, port and Cointreau, with a fruity pineapple finish. Yes, Hemingway also was here.

92 VIP HAVANA
Calle 9 no 454
entre E y F
Vedado ③
+53 7832 0178
www.viphavana454.com

Everybody is welcome in this modern, avant-gardist bar. Silent movies are projected on a large screen with accompanying music. You can also eat here. This upmarket restaurant specializes in rice and seafood. Elegant and luxurious.

93 **BOLABANA**
Calle 39 esq 50
Playa ⑤
+53 5294 3572

A new contemporary bar with a 'Miami'-style decoration. A trendy location near La Tropical, where hipsters meet the Havana farandula.

94 **SANGRI-LA**
Avenida 21
entre 36 y 42
Miramar ⑤
+53 5264 8343

The place to see singer Leoni Torres on Tuesdays. As a result, this club has become a well-known place. It alternates between private parties and regular events. Excellent gin and tonic.

95 **BAR DOS HERMANOS**
Avenida del Puerto
no 304 esq Sol
Habana Vieja ①
+53 7861 3514

Bar Dos Hermanos is located opposite Sierra Maestra terminal. This mojito bar was recently renovated. Hemingway also frequented this bar. Other important guests were Frederico Garcia Lorca and Marlon Brando. Open 24/7.

91 SLOPPY JOE'S

50 PLACES TO SHOP

———————

The 5 best places for
CUBAN MUSIC

96 **HABANA SÍ**

Calle 23 y L
Vedado ③
+53 7838 3181

One of the best places to buy Cuban music. The CDs are organized by musical genre, rumba, salsa and trova. Do take a look at their section of live DVDs and books. Besides music you can also buy souvenirs here. Everything is decorated with copies of paintings in the Museo de Bellas Artes.

97 **CASA DE LA MÚSICA EGREM**

Calle 20 no 3309
Miramar ⑤
+53 7204 0447
www.egrem.com.cu

Egrem, the national recording company, has the largest collection of music, CDs and DVDs. If you want to buy salsa, pick up a disc or two by Los Van Van or NG La Banda. Jazz fans will prefersome Chucho Valdes with Irakere, and Gonzalo Rubalcaba. Looking for Nueva Trova you'll definitely stock up on Pablo Milanes and Silvio Rodriguez. If you're more into son, choose classic releases by Beny Moré or look for Compay Segundo, Omara Portuondo and Eliades Ochoa. If it's Afro-Cuban sounds you're after, you'll love Yoruba Andabo. Go for rap and R&B by Dany Suarez and Telmary, reggaeton by El Micha and Los 4.

98 **SERIOSHA**

Neptuno entre
San Nicolas
y Manrique
Centro Habana ②

If you are a vinyl lover, this is the place to go. Cuban son, salsa, jazz, funk, mambo and more plus a good international section. Check the quality before buying. You will find treasures here. Start digging in Aladdin's cave.

99 **LONGINA MÚSICA**

Obispo entre Habana
y Compostela
Habana Vieja ①

We dare you to try and walk past this tiny store in bustling Obispo Street. The speakers which play tempting music will lure you inside. They sell a good selection of CDs as well as small percussion instruments including *maracas*, *bongos*, *guiros* and so on.

100 **ARTEHABANA**

San Rafael y Industria
Centro Habana ②

This is the biggest shop of Artex in Havana. Artex is the principal promotor of arts and literature. This shop stores a lot including books, clothes, decorative objects and, that's why I mention it in this section, a good music selection.

98 SERIOSHA

The 5 best places for
ORIGINAL SOUVENIRS
and more

**101 CLANDESTINA
99% DISEÑO CUBANO**

Villegas no 403 entre
Teniente Rey y Muralla
Habana Vieja ①
+53 5381 4802
www.clandestinacuba.com

Clandestina is a Cuban design brand. Graphic and industrial design, textile or digital. Imagination and creativity by young Cubans who make toys, sombreros, souvenirs, fashion, posters, and so on which you can buy in this studio-shop. My favourites are the tote bags which read 'Actually I'm in Havana'.

102 COSITASS

Avenida 3ra no 2804
entre 28 y 30
Miramar ⑤

In this shop in an old garage you will find charming little objects and the perfect gifts. From lamps to boxes, decorative objects and posters as well as flowerpots and even fountains. All the items are unique. Everything is handmade so no item is identical. Drink a coffee in the Cositass café next door.

**103 ANTIQUES CASA
DE BELKYS**

Calle 2 no 607
entre 25 y 27
Vedado ③

For true lovers of antiques. At Casa de Belkys you will find a large amount of vintage items, nic nacs and glassware on display.

104 PISCOLABIS BAZAR-CAFÉ

San Ignacio no 75
entre Callejon del
Chorro y O'Reilly
Habana Vieja ①
+53 5843 3219
*www.piscolabis
habana.com*

Piscolabis is a unique bazar with a small café. The result is a cosy atmosphere with designer and handcrafted items and original souvenirs of Havana. If you're hesitating about what to buy, sit down and drink a Cuban coffee or fruit shake while you mull it over.

105 CONGA

Avenida 3ra
entre 16 y 18
Miramar ⑤

A paradise for young Cuban designers, which sells jewels, bags, decorative items and so on. This little shop is called Conga referring to the Conga Santiaguera and its mixed rhythms, with people of all colors from different backgrounds starting to dance together when the musicians begin to play in the street. That's what you'll find in the shop: various styles and materials.

101 CLANDESTINA

5
MUST-BUYS
in Havana

---

106 ZULU BOLSOS DE PIEL

Fermando Fuero
no 104
Habana Vieja ①

Zulu bolsos is a local business founded by Zulueta Sardiñas. Purses, bags, wallets and more, of unique and exceptional quality. The designs are contemporary, elegant and timeless. Everything is made in Havana from recycled leather.

107 ALMA

Calle 18 no 314
entre 3ra y 5ta
Miramar ⑤
+53 5264 0660
www.almacubashop.com

The owner Alexandra Oppman has a keen eye and has curated a selection of local favourites you will want to take home, from simple necklaces to clever clutches. I'm a big fan of the paper note cards, bookmarks and notebooks.

108 MEMORIAS LIBRERÍA

Ánimas no 57
entre Prado y Zulueta
Centro Habana ②
+53 7862 5153
www.tiendamemorias.com

This is the leading old bookstore in Havana. Movie and political posters, baseball memorabilia, old China cups, fountain pens, old panoramic photos, books and magazines like Bohemia. Everything is nicely organized which makes for pleasant browsing. The owners of the place are friendly and helpful.

109 ESTUDIO CLEO

Calle I no 511 apto 1
entre 23 y 25
Vedado ③
+53 7832 3765

Estudio Cleo is situated in a beautiful and luminous Vedado house. Creative and original souvenirs, a wide selection of inspiring objects. It's impossible not to buy something. We guarantee you will only leave empty-handed if everything is sold out and they are waiting for new arrivals.

110 HABANA 1791

Mercaderes no 156
esq Obrapía
Habana Vieja ①
+53 7861 3525

Handmade perfumes from tropical flowers and plant oils. You can combine several ingredients yourself to create your own fragrance but first the alchemist-perfumer will sit down for a chat with you to find out more about your state of mind and character. There are over 300 basic aromas.

109 ESTUDIO CLEO

The 5 most charming places for
CUBAN FASHION

111 CAFÉ & BOUTIQUE JACQUELINE FUMERO

Compostela no 1
esq Cuarteles
Habana Vieja ①
+53 7862 6562

Exquisite fashionwear by internationally acclaimed designer Jacqueline Fumero. The shop also has a chic lounge and terrace where you can while away the time enjoying a refreshing sangria with pineapple and rum.

112 MODAS RAQUEL ATELIER CAFÉ

San Rafael
esq Consulado
Centro Habana ②
+53 7863 9380

Dresses in all colors of the rainbow and different models. The atelier is at the back of the store, which is quite handy because if you want to buy a dress that needs a small adjustment they'll do it right away.

113 EL QUITRIN

Obispo esq San Ignacio
Habana Vieja ①
+53 7862 0810

Here they sell embroideries and lace, chic blouses and skirts. For men you can buy the typical Cuban *guayaberas*, Cuban cotton shirts to beat the heat. They usually have four buttoned pockets and are embroidered with twin, vertical stripes down the front. Also check the men's collection at Guayabera Habanera, Tacó no 20 entre O'Reilly and Empedrado, Habana Vieja.

114 NOVATOR

Obispo no 365
esq Compostela
Habana Vieja ①
+53 7861 5292

The place to go for hats because that is their speciality. Their range is limited but interesting. They mainly sell sombreros in Panama and jipijapa style. The staff helps you make the right choice, but above all, they make sure you leave with the right size.

115 LA MAISON

Calle 16 no 701
esq Avenida 7ma
Miramar ⑤
+53 7204 1543
+53 7204 1541

This luxurious residence was built in 1946. It first served as a boarding house for students, after which it was refurbished in 1984 and 1986. This elegant place is multifunctional. Here you can buy clothes, jewels and perfume. At night there are fashion shows in the patio. It also has a coffee shop, restaurant, piano bar, a club upstairs and a swimming pool. Lovely garden.

111 JACQUELINE FUMERO

The 5 best places for
CIGARS and RUM

116 MUSEO DEL TABACO
Mercaderes no 120
Habana Vieja ⓘ
+53 7861 5795

This museum, founded in 1993, tells the history of tobacco and aims to conserve tobacco culture. It displays smoking paraphernalia and has a small cigar shop with *puros* of great quality. A small room is dedicated to my favourite person, the 'reader of the tobacco factory'. This tradition started in 1865 in the El Fígaro tobacco factory, on the initiative of a politician and the foreman. They devised this to make the long days in the factory more pleasant. Soon every Cuban tobacco factory installed a small platform, with a chair, from which the reader would read the daily news and literary works. Some of the cigars were even named after literary heroes.

117 CASA DEL HABANO
HOTEL CONDE
DE VILLANUEVA
Mercaderes no 202
Habana Vieja ⓘ
+53 7862 9293

Situated in the Hotel Conde de Villanueva in the historic city center. You have to walk through a splendid patio to get to the Casa del Habano. Once there, it's like being part of a secret because of the atmosphere they create.

118 FÁBRICA DE TABACO H. UPMANN

FORMERLY THE FABRICA ROMEO Y JULIETA

Padre Varela no 852
esq Peñalver
Centro Habana ②
+53 7878 1059

This famous cigar factory was established in 1873 by two Spaniards. It passed into the hands of José Rodriguez, who was passionate about cigars, in 1900. He bought the Capulet palace in Verona, where Romeo seduced Julieta and opened a cigar shop there too. Guided tours are available. You can even hear the reader outside of the factory. The Romeo y Julieta is the most distributed Cuban cigar in the world, after the Montecristo.

119 CASA DEL HABANO

5ta Avenida no 1407
entre 14 y 16
Miramar ⑤
+53 7204 7973

Impressive cigar shop in a posh mansion, with a wide range of brands, including some rare and collectible cigars. The experienced staff knows its merchandise well. Take all the time you need. You should definitely try a peppery and fresh 'Hoyo de Monterrey Epicure no 2' or the spicy and flavorful 'Ramon Allones'.

120 CASA DEL RON Y DEL TABACO CUBANO

Obispo entre Bernaza
y Avenida de Belgica
Habana Vieja ①
+53 7866 0911

One of the best selections of rum under one roof in whole Havana and a decent range of Habanos. Buy a 'Havana Club Selección de los Maestros' for a taste of Cuba at home or a 'Legendario Dorado' and a 'Cubay Oscuro' to share with your friends.

The 5 best places for
POSTCARDS, POSTERS
and PHOTOGRAPHS

121 MODERNA POESÍA

Obispo esq Bernaza
Habana Vieja ①
+53 7861 6983

The largest bookstore of Havana hides behind this gigantic Art Deco façade from 1938. Poetry, academic books and political and social works. The most interesting are the beautiful black and white postcards you can buy at the entrance, stamp included.

122 SHOP OF THE MUSEO DE BELLAS ARTES

Trocadero entre
Agramonte and
Monserrate
Centro Habana ②
www.bellesartes.cult.cu

On the ground floor of the museum there's a small shop with a good selection of art books and documentaries on DVD. Nice posters and postcards. Also small souvenirs including magnets and bookmarks.

123 INSTITUTO CUBANO DEL ARTE E INDUSTRIA CINEMATOGRAFICOS

Calle 23 entre 10 y 12
Vedado ③

Cuban movie posters are little works of art. Their style is exactly the opposite of Hollywood posters. The ICAIC is the best place to buy them because of the wide selection they offer. You will find the whole collection at the back of the Fresa y Chocolate-café. They also have an excellent DVD selection.

124 GALERÍA ROBERTO SALAS

Calle 30 no 3709
entre 37 y 39
Playa ⑤
+53 7206 5213

Roberto Salas documented the revolution from the Sierra Maestra until the Bay of Pigs, as well as the only known meeting between Fidel Castro and Ernest Hemingway. His artistry and great ability to capture the common people led to over 40 solo exhibitions worldwide. In the studio of photographer Roberto Salas you can buy his iconic images of Havana in the fifties.

125 ANDARE BAZAR DE ARTE

YARA CINEMA
Esq Calle 23 y L
Vedado ③

You'll find this shop inside the Yara cinema. Even if you didn't plan go to the movies, this is a perfect reason to enter the cinema, to buy some antique postcards and Cuban movie posters

121 LA MODERNA POESÍA

The 5 most interesting
BOOKSHOPS

---

126 **PLAZA DE ARMAS**
Habana Vieja ①

Havana's biggest second-hand book fair. Look for a book that explains the revolution using Panini-type stickers. It was developed to teach children about the revolution, while entertaining them as they collected the stickers. Che Guevara, Camillo Cienfuegos, Fidel Castro: you'll find them all in this book.

127 **LIBRERÍA FERNANDO ORTIZ**
Calle L esq Calle 27
Vedado ③
+53 8329653

This bookshop, which is just a stone's throw from the university, is named after Fernando Ortiz Fernández, a prominent Cuban anthropologist, essayist and expert of Afro-Cuban culture. A good selection of essays and literature and a limited number of books in English.

128 **LIBRERÍA FAYAD JAMÍS**
Obispo no 261
entre Cuba y Aguiar
Habana Vieja ①

This beautifully restored bookshop with wooden pillars and a wooden balcony has the largest selection of books in Havana. Here you pay in national Pesos which makes it cheap for visitors.

129 LIBRERÍA CENTENARIO DEL APÓSTOL

Calle 25 no 164
entre Infanta y O
Vedado ③
+53 7870 7220

Tons of used books. You'll find interesting things here. The staff like to give some recommendations. This bookshop is also a meeting place, where you will always end up meeting someone nice for a book chat.

130 PALACIO DEL SEGUNDO CABO

O'Reilly no 4 esq Cuba
Habana Vieja ①
www.segundocabo.ohc.cu

Built in 1770 as the residence of the Spanish vice-governor. After several incarnations as a post office, Palace of the Senate, the Supreme Court and the National Academy of Arts and Literature, the building is now home to a well-stocked bookstore. Lovers of pop art should visit the space dedicated to Cuban painter Raùl Martinez.

126 PLAZA DE ARMAS

The 5 best places to
BUY ART

131 ARTE MALECÓN
Calle D entre 1ra y 3ra
Vedado ③

Quality paintings, ceramics and other handicrafts, including items engraved or printed with images of the Museo de Bellas Artes. Also has a bar and café.

132 GALERÍA GALIANO
Galiano no 256
entre Concordia
y Neptuno
Centro Habana ②
+53 7860 0224
www.galeriagaliano.com

There are not many places like this one in Centro Habana. They organize several exhibitions with works by interesting young contemporary artists here. The influence of major masters is noticeable here, but there is always margin for innovation.

133 GALERÍA LA ACACIA
San Martin 114
entre Industria
y Consulado
Centro Habana ②

Just behind de Gran Teatro de la Habana, this gallery sells artwork by contemporary Cuban creators including Zaida del Rio. This gallery takes care of all the export formalities. There's a space for permanent and temporary exhibitions. Works by Wifredo Lam, Amelia Peáez and René Portocarrero have been exhibited here.

134 GALERÍA ORIGENES

Paseo de Martí no 458
entre San Rafael
y San Martin
Centro Habana ②
+53 7863 6690

Forming part of the Gran Teatro complex, across the Parque Central, this gallery has high ceilings, marble floors and neo-baroque detailing. Work of a high standard and all paintings and sculptures are available for sale. They arrange the paperwork for you.

135 GALERÍA VICTOR MANUEL

San Ignacio no 56
Plaza de la Catedral
Habana Vieja ①
+53 7861 2955

This galería is situated in an old colonial mansion in the historic center and pays tribute to the painting of the Gitana Tropical, Victor Manuel García. The merchandise is of a relatively high standard, including Art Nouveau lamps, photographs of Havana and sculptures.

The 5 cosiest
STREET MARKETS

---

136 **AGROMERCADO 19 Y B**
Calle 19 y B
Vedado ③

Farmers who have supplied their quota to the government may sell their surplus produce in *agromercados* or farmer's markets. This market sells fruit and vegetables as well as meat, rice and beans. One of the best-stocked open-air vegetable markets in the city.

137 **MERCADO EGIDO**
Avenida de Belgica
entre Corrales
y Apodaca
Habana Vieja ①

You can buy flowers at the entrance and fruit and vegetables, beans, rice, honey, spices in the huge indoor market. There are painted inscriptions on the walls such as *'la arcilla fundamental de nuestra obra es la juventud'*.

138 **AGROMERCADO 27 Y A**
Esq Calle 27 y A
Vedado ③

This is a mid-sized market in Vedado. Fruit and vegetables, fresh juice and fried food. So if you don't have a kitchen grab some snacks here and enjoy a freshly squeezed mango juice as you stroll around the city. In Centro Habana you can head over to the agromercado en Animas entre Aramburu y Soledad.

139 TULIPAN MARKET

Esq Tulipan y Marino
Plaza de la Revolución
Nuevo Vedado ④

This large market is situated to the south of Vedado, near Plaza de la Revolución. People travel from all over to come to this market because the prices are the cheapest here. There are also several independent streetfood vendors. In the morning you will often see people have their breakfast here on their way in to work.

140 TIENDA DE MARCO POLO, EL CAMINO DE LAS ESPECIAS

Mercaderes 111
entre Obispo y
Obrapía
Habana Vieja ①

This small shop sells various aromatic and medicinal herbs and spices. You can buy cumin (which is a popular ingredient with Habaneros), cinnamon, thyme and other herbs here to season your dishes. The mix of all these spices combines into an incredible scent, which wafts around the shop.

136 AGROMERCADO 19 Y B

137 MERCADO EGIDO

5 typical
HANDICRAFT MARKETS
and shops to buy coffee

---

141 CENTRO CULTURAL ANTIGUOS DE ALMACENES DE DEPÓSITO SAN JOSÉ

Avenida del Puerto
entre Habana y Cuba
Habana Vieja ①

The Feria de San José is a giant warehouse facing the sea. Here you can find all the typical souvenirs under one roof. Everything you can think of with a Che on it, cigars, jewels, clothes, paintings. Take advantage of the opportunity to buy some Nauta cards (to go online). The wait is never too long in the Etecsa office.

142 PALACIO DE ARTESANÍA

Cuba no 64 entre
Cuarteles y Peña Pobre
Habana Vieja ①

A colonial palace where you can buy several things. There's a section dedicated to typical musical instruments used to play traditional Cuban music. Also a good selection of Cuban handicrafts, clothing and jewellery. There's also a restaurant, bar and ice cream shop.

143 MERCADO LA RAMPA LA FERIA DE 23

Calle 23 entre M y N
Vedado ③

Small craft market selling imported clothes, handmade leather items and wood carvings. Also check the Feria de Artesania at Malecón entre D y E, Vedado.

144 CAFÉ EL ESCORIAL

Plaza Vieja
Mercaderes no 317
Habana Vieja ①
+53 7868 3545

Freshly roasted coffee beans, grown in Escambray, a mountainous area in central Cuba, are available for purchase here. Buy them to take that excellent Cuban coffee flavor home with you. Since there's always a lot of people in line to buy coffee, sit down, put in your request and order a coffee on the terrace. Besides the usual latte, cappuccino or espresso, part of the menu also includes coffees mixed with all kind of rums and other liquors.

145 CASA DEL HABANO

HOTEL NACIONAL
Calle O esq 21
Vedado ③
+53 7836 3564

Make sure to stop here and buy tons of coffee before leaving Havana. Go to the basement to buy the best and most addictive there is. A bit expensive but worth it: 'Montecristo Deleggend', a mountain coffee from the Sierra Maestra. Do also try 'Cohiba Atmosphere', a coffee from El Nicho. Upstairs you can stock up on Arriero and Serrano coffee. Bags of one kilo for yourself and small bags as gifts for your coffee-loving friends.

CASA DE LA AMISTAD

25 BUILDINGS
TO ADMIRE

The 5 most stunning
ART DECO BUILDINGS

---

146 EDIFICIO BACARDI
Monserrate no 261
entre Empedrado
y San Juan de Dios
Centro Habana ②

This skyscraper, which was built in 1930 by Esteban Rodriguez Castells, Rafael Fernandez Ruenes and José Menendez, is a stunning art deco landmark. Its façade is made of red granite and local limestone, with terracotta panels of naked nymphs by Maxfield Parrish, and is topped with the iconic bat motif. Head up to the top tower for a 360°-view. Head over to the terrace of Hotel Plaza, across the street, for a full view of the building.

147 EDIFICIO LOPEZ SERRANO
Calle 13 no 108 esq L
Vedado ③

Considered the first Cuban skyscraper. It featured layered fittings in order to let the air and light in. The façade's linear and geometric lines are enhanced by the Moroccan red marble of the interior, the decorative large flowerpots, ceiling lamps and doors to lifts and apartments.

148 CINE ASTRAL
Infanta no 501
esq San Martin
Centro Habana ②

Cine Astral is only a few blocks from Cine Infanta. It was built in a streamlined late art deco style and opened in 1950 with a seating capacity of 2400.

149 CINE-TEATRO SIERRA MAESTRA (FORMER TEATRO LUTGARDITA)

Calzada de Bejucal
no 30901
Reparto Lutgardita -
Rancho Boyeros

This theater opened in 1932 and has a modest art deco exterior. The interior combines Central American themes including pre-Columbian iconography and landscape murals featuring Mayan temples. Visit every Sunday for the Parranda Campesina (traditional music, dancing, storytelling and comedy).

150 EDIFICIO SOLIMAR

Soledad no 205
esq San Lázaro
Centro Habana ②

A striking art deco building built by Manuel Copado in 1944. This huge apartment complex has curved balconies that wrap around the building, resembling the ocean's waves. A good example of expressionist modern architecture.

146 EDIFICIO BACARDI

150 EDIFICIO SOLIMAR

5 more

ART DECO HOUSES

151 CASA DE LA AMISTAD

Paseo de Martí no 406
entre 17 y 19
Vedado ③
+53 7831 2823

A perfect example of an early twentieth-century residential art deco interior. The building was built by two lovebirds. Catalina Lasa was stuck in a loveless marriage with a rich aristocrat. She fell in love with another man, the land-owner Juan Pedro Baró in 1905. The lovers escaped to Paris to continue their love affair as there were no divorce laws in Cuba at the time. They returned to Cuba in 1917 after divorce became legal. Baró built Catalina a neo-classical/Italian Renaissance villa on Vedado's grand avenue, painting it pink, her favourite color. When she died in 1930 Baró returned to France. Nowadays it is home to the Casa de la Amistad. Various activities are organized here in order to promote cultural exchanges. Now there's a weekly Chan Chan night in his honour. The art deco dining room with its Lalique glass panels now is home to a restaurant called Primavera.

151 CASA DE LA AMISTAD

152 CASA DE LAS AMERICAS

Avenida 3ra no 52
esq G
Vedado ③
+53 7838 2707
*www.casadelas
americas.org*

Resembling a vertical church, this building, which was built in 1947, has a triple telescopic clock tower, which was added in 1953. Take a look at the art deco details in the relief above the canopy entrance, the cupola and the four-faced clock. The geometric vertical lines and recesses are characteristics of the streamlined art deco architecture that was so popular in Havana two decades earlier. Casa de las America, founded in 1959, promotes Latin American literature and art.

153 GRAN TEMPLO MASÓNICO DE CUBA

Avenida Salvador
Allende no 508
Centro Habana ②

The Gran Templo Masónico by Emilio Vasconcelos, which was built in 1955, is one of his last modern works. By then the more rational, less flamboyant second modern movement was becoming increasingly popular.

154 HOSPITAL MUNICIPAL DE MATERNIDAD AMÉRICA ARIAS

Avenida G no 240
entre 9 y Línea
Vedado ③

This hospital, which the locals also call la Maternidad de Línea, is one of the first art deco buildings to be built in Havana. It was designed in 1930 by the architects Govantes and Cabaroccas. The building is vertically oriented and has a typical art deco façade with decorative art deco elements. We definitely recommend walking past this building and taking some time to marvel at it.

155 **CASA DE JULIA TARAFA**
Calle 8 no 510
entre Avenida 5ta y
Avenida 7ta
Miramar ⑤

This private house was designed by Angel de Zárraga in 1933. Art deco prospered at a time of commercial success (sugar trade). The combination of pastels with whimsical motifs creates a tropical deco look.

152 CASA DE LAS AMERICAS

The 5 best places to find
INTERESTING ARCHITECTURE

156 GRAN TEATRO

Paseo de Martí
esq San Rafael
Centro Habana ②
+53 7861 3077

In 1938, a Belgian architect started to build this theater, which is a neo-baroque edifice with corner towers topped with angels and which also features sculptures of the muses of charity, education, music and theater. It is now home to the National Ballet of Cuba.

157 TROPICANA

Calle 72 no 4504
entre 41 y 43
Marianao
+53 7267 1010
www.cabaret-
tropicana.com

Built around trees and considered the masterpiece of Cuban architect Max Borges, this open air theater is an example of fifties modernism. Borges added the famous geometric sculpture that still forms the backdrop to the main stage in the outdoor salon Bajo las Estrellas.

158 CASA DE LAS TEJAS VERDES

Calle 2 entre 3ra y 5ta
Miramar ⑤
+53 7212 5282

Named after the green tiles which were used for the roof. Unique in Cuba as it is the only example of German renaissance. The house now serves as center for the promotion and study of urban planning, modern architecture and interior design.

159 ISA

Calle 120 no 1110
entre 9na y 13
Playa ⑤
+53 7208 9771
www.isa.cult.cu

Designed by three rebel architects, this art school project was soon stopped because it was considered too avant-garde. The controversial, papaya-shaped fountain in front of the building and one of the painting studio pavilions which has a glass skylight refer to the female body. While the school did open, the complex soon fell into disrepair. In 2001 the government asked the three architects to complete the project.

160 FOCSA

Calle 17, 19, M y N
Vedado ③

One of the seven wonders of the world by a Cuban genius. This skyscraper, completed in 1956, marked the beginning of an era of Cuban skyscrapers. It is 121 meters tall and has 39 floors and 373 apartments. Loosely based on a design by Le Corbusier.

158 CASA DE LAS TEJAS VERDES

5 giants of
SPORTS
INFRASTRUCTURE

161 CIUDAD DEPORTIVA

Rancho Boyeros
esq Via Blanca
Cerro ④

El Coliseo has become an urban landmark just because of its spectacular form. It also represents a milestone in terms of construction and is a showcase for the high quality contracting work that was performed at the time. The stadium can seat up to 15.000 spectators. The audience can be evacuated in under ten minutes thanks to two wide ramps that lead to the ground level.

162 NAUTICAL CLUB

5ta Avenida y 152
Miramar ⑤
+53 7242718

The Nautical Club was built in the twenties. By the fifties, the membership had increased significantly, requiring the club to expand. Max Borges designed an enormous set of porticos covered by vaults. The architectonic structure is establishing an almost literal analogy with the waves of the sea nearby.

163 ESTADIO PANAMERICANO

Via Monumental, km 4
(Cojímar)

Inaugurated in 1991 for the Pan American games. Seating for up to 35.000 people.

164 ESTADIO LATINOAMERICANO

Zequera no 312
Cerro ④

This complex can accommodate up to 55.000 spectators and has coffee shops, conference rooms, broadcasting and press boxes and medical services. Baseball was introduced in Cuba at the end of the nineteenth century and is currently the most popular sport in the country. The stadium hosts National League matches and Cuba's most important international games.

165 SALA POLIVALENTE KID CHOCOLATE

Paseo de Martí
y Teniente Rey
Habana Vieja ①
+53 7861 1546

This is one of the 67 especially built facilities for the Havana 1991 Pan American games. It was named after Eligio Sardeñas, also known as Kid Chocolate, Cuba's finest amateur boxer ever.

161 CIUDAD DEPORTIVA

5 must-visit
LIBRARIES, THEATERS
and a BOOKSHOP

166 **LIBRARY OF THE ECONOMIC SOCIETY OF FRIENDS OF THE COUNTRY**
Carlos III no 710
entre Soledad
y Castillejo
Centro Habana ②

The overall message of this building is one of austerity, conveyed by the lofty portico and the rectangular volume with only a few openings. The book depot tower which has rows of windows, which resemble slits, serves as the rear façade. The building has an inviting, central patio full of lush greenery. Built by Govantes and Cabaroccas.

167 **BIBLIOTECA NACIONAL JOSÉ MARTÍ**
Avenida Independencia
esq 20 de Mayo
Vedado ③
+53 7855 5442
www.bnjm.cu

This impressive-looking library rizes up on the edge of Plaza de la Revolución and is a good example of modern architecture. This tower overlooks part of Havana and is divided into four reading rooms, two libraries, one theater, three galleries, a video projection room, a cafeteria and a special service for researchers.

168 **MODERNA POESÍA**
Obispo y Bernaza
Habana Vieja ①
+53 7861 6983

This art deco building is now a book-store but originally it was a publishing house owned by José López Serrano and built in 1935.

169 **TEATRO AMÉRICA**
Galiano no 253 entre
Neptuno y Concordia
Centro Habana ②
+53 7862 5416

Teatro América was designed by Fernando Martinez Campos and Pascual de Rojas and has contrasting green-and-white lines and recessed windows. The symmetrical elegant façade and the zodiac signs in the main loby are a good example of (late) art deco. The stage is shell-shaped and the auditorium has more than hundred seats.

170 **TEATRO FAUSTO**
Paseo de Martí
esq Colón
Centro Habana ②

Designed by Saturnino Parajón. The theater was built on the foundations of an old theater and completed in 1938. In 1941, Parajón received the Architectural Association's Gold Medal for his design. The classic art deco façade is clad with a mixture of white cement and stone dust which changes color when illuminated with incandescent gas tubes.

169 TEATRO AMÉRICA

170 TEATRO FAUSTO

BIBLIOTECA NACIONAL JOSÉ MARTÍ

85 PLACES
TO DISCOVER
LA HABANA

The 5 best
SONGS
about Havana

---

171 EL SOLAR DE LA CALIFORNIA
ISSAC DELGADO

Put this song on and you will immediately book tickets to leave for Havana. Listen carefully to the words. First we walk through Calle 23 in Vedado to head in to Centro Habana with the invitation *"si quieres conocer"*. *"La verdadera Habana"*, where we call each other *"primo"* and *"hermano"*, where people make love in colors, where they play dominos, where cucurucho is sold (a delicacy from Baracoa), and where several people live together in a solar. A wonderful song that is so true to life.

172 LA HABANA ME LLAMA
MANOLITO SIMONET Y SU TRABUCO

"La Habana tiene un swing es por eso que se llama la Habana", says the refrain of this song. This means everything and nothing. Havana has swing and soon you too will agree that this is true. You don't always need many words to bring a message.

173 LA HABANA NO AGUANTO MÁS
LOS VAN VAN

This song was written by Juan Formell and says that Havana is filling up and can no longer cope, that everyone wants to be here. The Cubans from the other provinces or Cubans who already have family members living there with the rest wanting to follow. As is the case with many refrains and lyrics from the songs of Los Van Van, this lyric also became a saying, a proverb.

174 SABANAS BLANCAS
GERARDO ALFONSO

A tribute to Havana written and sung by the singer-songwriter Gerardo Alfonso. The title refers to the white sheets that dry on the balconies. He references centrally located places such as the cathedral and the port as well as various neighborhoods such as Regla, Nuevo Vedado and la Virgen del Camino.

175 MI HABANA (LA HABANA NO MUERO)
TRAJE NUEVO

This song by the Cuban group Traje Nuevo refers to the cannon which is fired every day at 9 pm precisely at Morro Fortress. *"Sigue soñando con el cañon de las 9, la Habana vive, la Habana no muero"*. Havana lives on, even after the cannon is fired, Havana lives day and night. They often say that NY is the city that never sleeps but this also applies to Havana.

The 5 best
M O V I E S
and their places in Havana

---

176 VAMPIROS EN LA HABANA
CINÉ PAYRET
Paseo de Martí
no 503-513
Habana Vieja ①

Vampiros en la Habana is an animated masterpiece by Juan Padrón. Clandestine vampire communities are battling to find a magic potion. When Werner Amadeus von Dracula, the son of Count Dracula, arrives in Cuba as a refugee, he develops a magic potion that allows vampires to withstand the light. He tests this on his unsuspecting cousin, the hip trumpet player Pepito. He is finally informed of what is going on and from then on hides in the Payret cinema where they show Dracula.

177 HABANA BLUES
Rooftop Calle 13
y Calle 8
Vedado ③

With *Habana Blues*, the director Benito Zambrano juxtaposes the story of the two musicians Ruy and Tito and their daily life, alongside the corresponding problems in Cuba. Many snapshots of streets, of the rooftops and inhabitants of Havana. The emphasis is placed on the ambivalence and the contradictions, also largely with the music.

178 CHICO Y RITA
TROPICANA

Calle 72 no 4504
entre 41 y 43
Marianao

This visually inventive animated film by Fernando Trueba is inspired by the life of the pianist Bebo Valdes. Besides being a lovely film, it also has an excellent soundtrack with his compositions. This is the musical Havana of the fifties, where the jazz singer Rita and the pianist Chico meet at the Tropicana cabaret.

179 FRESA Y CHOCOLATE
LA GUARIDA

Concordia no 418
entre Gervasio
y Escobar
Centro Habana ②

Fresa y chocolate portrays the story of Diego, a homosexual artist and David, who plans to spy on Diego. The contemporary restaurant La Guarida serves as Diego's apartment in the film. The entire setting symbolizes the claustrophobic hiding and being stuck in a closed system, as well as the belief in the opportunities for development and change towards more tolerance and openness.

180 MIEL PARA OSHÚN
HOTEL NACIONAL

Calle 21 y O
Vedado ③

This film by Humberto Solas tells the story of a young boy, Roberto, who was taken to the United States by his father at the age of seven. Once grown up, he returned to Havana to visit his mother. The result was an encounter with his native Cuba and identity.

The 5 best types of
TRANSPORT TO USE

181 ALMENDRÓN OR MAQUINA

El almendrón or *maquina* refers to the cars of the fifties and sixties used as public transport. Usually you pay 10 Pesos moneda nacional, depending on the distance. Ford, Chevrolet, Buick or Cadillac. Some are in better shape than others. You always share a taxi, the taxi does not leave if it is not full. If you want to experience how Habaneros get from one point to another, take the almendrón for a day.

182 COCO TAXI

Car rickshaw with seats for two passengers, in an egg/coconut form. The color of the Coco Taxi for tourists is always yellow. Cubans take the black one. Pay with CUC. Cheaper than a taxi, interesting for short distances.

182 **COCO TAXI**

181 **ALMENDRÓN**

183 BICITAXI

The bicitaxi is a popular form of transport used by the locals with two seats for passengers. They all have sound systems. The bicitaxi dates from the special period. Pedal power was a resourceful response to the lack of fuel.

184 LADA
TAXI PARTICULAR

Is cheaper than the yellow taxi. You will pay 5 or 6 CUC for the journey from Habana Vieja to Vedado. *"No tire las puertas"* is what the driver will tell you. Don't slam the door. Close them softly instead.

185 GUAGUA

La guagua means bus. The buses are always too full because of the lack of public transport. People wait in line to get on the bus. Ask who's last when you join the queue: *"Quien es el ultimo?"*.

183 BICITAXI ON O'REILLY

Meet 5
SANTOS
in the Museum of the Orishas

Prado no 615 entre
Monte y Dragones
Habana Vieja ①
+53 7863 5953
www.yorubacuba.org

186 OCHÚN

Ochún is the youngest of all Orishas. She is syncretized with the Virgen de la Caridad del Cobre, Cuba's patron saint. This makes her special to Cubans, they celebrate her feast on 8 September, which is considered a major holiday. Her colors are yellow and gold. Ochún is the goddess of love, her seductive and sensual power encapsulates the feminine ideal.

187 YEMAYÁ

Sister of Ochún. They have a close relationship. Yemayá is a mature motherly type who watches over children and protects babies in the womb. She is the great mother that rules over the seas. Her colors are blue and white.

188 **CHANGÓ**

Changó is the owner of fire, lightening, thunder and war but he is also the patron of music, drumming and dancing. He represents male beauty and virility. His colors are red and white.well as a world-class meal.

189 **ELEGUÁ**

He represents the beginning and the end of life, and the opening and closing of paths in life. Eleguá is always mentioned first in a ceremony because without his permission the doors to communication with the other orishas remains closed. He is syncretized with Jesus of Atocha, Saint Anthony of Padua and the Anima Sola. His colors are red and black.

190 **OBATALA**

He is the creator of earth and the sculptor of mankind. Obatalá is the owner of all things that are white, as well as the human head and all of its thoughts and dreams. Obatalá protects against blindness, paralysis and dementia.

The 5 best places to feel
'LA ALEGRÍA CUBANA'

191 **ARTE CORTE-PAPITO**
Aguiar no 10 entre
Peña Pobre y Avenida
de las Misiones
Habana Vieja ①
+53 7861 0202

Papito calls his hair salon and small museum an interactive monument. You can admire razors, old scissors and lots of other tools with a history while sitting in this one hundred-year-old barber's chair. The street is called *el Callejon de los Peluqueros*. Papito's passion and energy have helped create a trendy street, with various new businesses opening.

192 **PATIO DE LA RUMBA
EL GRAN PALENQUE**
Calle 4 no 103
entre 5ta y Calzada
Vedado ③
+53 7836 9075

Afro-Cuban religious and secular dance and drumming for three hours, on Saturdays from 3 till 6 pm. This is known as el Sabado de la Rumba, an event that is hosted by El Conjunto Folklórico Nacional de Cuba. Rumba, guaguancó and yambú. Great atmosphere with Cuban regulars, grandmothers, children, students, tourists, santeros, local neighbors. Listen to the rhythm of the congas and let the rhythm take you over. This is the real stuff.

193 SALÓN DE ENSAYO BENNY MORÉ

Neptuno no 960
entre Hospital
y Aramburu
Centro Habana ②

The rehearsal studio of the production house EGREM is located in this popular street in Centro Habana. The door is always open so walk by and listen to the music of some excellent groups playing son, guaracha or another type of traditional music.

194 PEÑA OBINI BATÁ

A folkloric percussion group, all women, playing batá drums, chéqueres, tumbadoras, cajones in addition to the singing, reciting and dancing. They play on Fridays at the Yoruba Center and on Saturdays at Casa de Africa.

195 CALLEJÓN DE HAMEL

Callejón de Hamel
entre Aramburu
y Hospital
Centro Habana ②

El Callejón de Hamel is a community project related to Afro-Cuban culture inspired by the painter, sculptor and muralist Salvador González Escalona. His goal was to bring new life to Cayo Hueso. The result is that there are a lot of street paintings that evoke African art, sculptures and installations of contemporary art. The roofs are covered with many colors, poetry, images. Go on Sunday during the rumba.

195 CALLEJÓN DE HAMEL

5 *of the best places to*
MEET LOCALS

---

196 MALECÓN

A 9-km stretch of pure Cuban soul. You have to have walked on the Malecón at least once and spent some time there to understand it. Lots of talking, drinking, kissing, having a good time close to the sea, where you unwind and escape from the warmth of the day. This is Havana.

197 LA RAMPA

La Rampa or Calle 23 is a very popular walk for Habaneros of all ages. There are bars, cafés, places to dance and cinemas. It's always crowded, so it is the perfect place to experience Havana's atmosphere. A year ago, they added Wi-Fi, so you can now connect with the world with a 2 CUC scratch card and by entering the login and password. Even Wi-Fi is a collective activity here.

196 MALECÓN

199 PARQUE CENTRAL

200 UNIVERSIDAD DE LA HABANA

198 COPPELIA

Calle 23 y L
Vedado ③
+53 7832 6184

Havana's Coppelia is one of the largest ice-cream parlors in the world. It opened in 1966 and became even more famous after being featured in the film *Fresa y Chocolate*. Coppelia was developed by Fidel Castro and his longtime secretary Célia Sanchez and named after her favorite ballet *Coppélia*. The queues are endless because Cubans love ice cream and they love this place.

199 PARQUE CENTRAL

Habana Vieja ①

A statue of José Martí stands in the middle of the park and is surrounded by 28 palm trees, in reference to his birthday on the 28th of January. This is a good place to sit and observe daily life in Havana. The *'esquina caliente'*, where men talk about *pelota* incessantly can be found on the left side of the park.

200 UNIVERSIDAD DE LA HABANA

Calle L y 27
Vedado ③
www.uh.cu

Located in the Vedado district, this university was founded in 1728. It is the oldest university of Cuba and one of the first in the Americas. It welcomes 30.000 students each year. You can choose to sit on the stairs of the main entrance and watch San Lázaro and the energy and speed of life or instead walk to the courtyard park where you can talk to the students.

5 of the most interesting
REVOLUTIONARY SITES

201 **PLAZA DE LA REVOLUCIÓN**

Paseo y Boyeros
Vedado ③

This esplanade has experienced every detailed step of the Revolution, starting with the literacy campaign and ending with the farewell ceremony dedicated to Che Guevara. It is also here that Fidel Castro held many of his (very long) speeches. On the façade of the Ministry of the Interior you can see a gigantic representation of Che, looking at the Revolution forever.

202 **MUSEO DE LA REVOLUCIÓN AND GRANMA MEMORIAL**

Refugio no 1
entre Monserrate
y Zulueta
Habana Vieja ①
+53 7862 4093

The rooms and area of this museum provide a vast and detailed panorama of the struggles of the Cuban people to achieve its complete sovereignty. In front of the building the visitor will be able to admire the tank used by Fidel Castro during the Bay of Pigs invasion as well as the Granma yacht in the space behind the museum. The Granma yacht transported Castro and his 82 men including Che Guevara, from Mexico to Cuba in 1956. A real treasure is el Salón de los Espejos, designed to resemble to a Palace de Versailles-room.

202 MUSEO DE LA REVOLUCIÓN

203 CENTRO DE ESTUDIOS CHE GUEVARA

Calle 47 no 772
entre Conill y Tulipan
Plaza de la Revolución
Vedado ③
+53 7881 4113
www.centroche.co.cu

The initiative for this centro de estudios was taken after a discussion between Aleida March, Che's second wife and Fidel Castro. This institution is based in Che's former home where he lived from 1962 until he left for Africa. The center is tasked with the study, the knowledge and distribution of the ideas of Che Guevara. It also offers visitors an insight into his life and work.

204 MUSEO DE COMANDANCIA DEL CHE

Fortaleza de San Carlos
de la Cabaña
Carretera del Cristo
Casablanca ①

Che Guevara worked in one of the buildings of la Cabaña from 3 January 1959 on. Today you can see a mock-up of his office and documentation about the time he spent there. Che fans will also be happy to take a closer look at a number of cult objects, such as Che's camera, backpack and binoculars. A map of the world charts Che's motor travels in Latin America as well as his official visits to Asia.

205 MUSEO CASA NATAL CAMILO CIENFUEGOS

Pocito no 228
esq Lawton
Diez de Octubre

Camilo Cienfuegos was born here on 6 February 1932. There are five small rooms you can visit. Explore his life, from his childhood until the last ten months of his life, through manuscripts, images and personal belongings of the commandant and his family. His sombrero can be found in the fifth room.

The 5 cosiest
PARKS and PLAZAS

---

206 PARQUE DE MIRAMAR
5ta Avenida
entre 24 y 26
Miramar ⑤

A quiet park with lovely trees where you can enjoy nature in the middle of an upmarket residential area. The perfect place to read a book in the shadow and escape the warmth of the sun. At the entrance of the park you can spot a statue of Mahatma Gandhi and one of Emilio Zapata, the leader of the Mexican Revolution, at the other end of the avenue.

207 PARQUE LUZ CABALLERO
Tacón entre Chacón
y Empedrado
Habana Vieja ①

This park is named after the Cuban intellectual, writer and philosopher José de la Luz y Caballero. He is also one of the co-founders of Cuban nationality. His statue is easy to recognize in this park. Use the benches to reflect on and search for intellectual impulses. The two busts at either end of the park represent the Cuban thinkers, Félix Varela, the father of the nation and José Antonio Saco.

208 PLAZA DE ARMAS
Habana Vieja ⓘ

This is the place where it all started. It was built in the sixteenth century and soon overrun by soldiers who liked to organize their exercises here. Hence its name, by the way. Subsequently several changes were made up to 1841. From then on the square remained unchanged. There is a garden in the center of the square, with a sculpture of Carlos Manuel de Céspedes.

209 PLAZUELA DEL ÁNGEL
Compostela
esq Cuarteles
Habana Vieja ⓘ

It is incredible to find such a lovely and tranquil beauty spot in bustling Habana Vieja. The sculpture of the literary figure Cecilia Valdés and the bust of her writer Cirilo Villaverde, have been installed in front of the church of el Santo Angel Custodio. José Martí, Alicia Alonso and la Milagrosa were all baptized here.

210 PARQUE ECOLÓGICO HANS CHRISTIAN ANDERSEN
Mercaderes entre
O'Reilly y Empedrado
Habana Vieja ⓘ

This park is dedicated to the writer Hans Christian Andersen, and you will also find a bust of the author here. It is a special place with exotic and traditional plants. They also grow medicinal plants and fruit trees here. There is a museum/auditorium where primary school children are taught more about nature and are involved in it, but the classes also specifically focus on the park and on what happens here.

The 5 most stunning
STATUES
of historical figures

---

211 **MONUMENTO LENIN**
Parque Lenin
Calle 100 y Cortina
de la Presa
Arroyo Naranjo
+53 7644 2721

Parque Lenin is dominated by the huge granite face of the Communist leader and thinker in Soviet-realist style, which was carved by I.E. Kerbel in 1982. There's also an inscription of Fidel Castro at the right side of the granite that says that Lenin was besides a politician also and always a man of revolutionary action.

212 **MEMORIAL A CELIA SÁNCHEZ MANDULEY**
Parque Lenin
Calle 100 y Cortina
de la Presa
Arroyo Naranjo
+53 7644 2721

Parque Lenin also contains a bronze figure of the revolutionary heroine Celia Sánchez Manduley. It was on her initiative that the park was built between 1969 and 1972. Celia Sánchez was a Cuban revolutionary, researcher and archivist. She worked as Secretary to the Presidency of the Council of Ministers, so she always worked closely with Fidel Castro. She served in the Council of State until her death due to lung cancer in 1980.

213 MONUMENTO A MÁXIMO GÓMEZ

Esq Malecón
y Paseo de Martí
Habana Vieja ①

This statue pays tribute to the Dominican war hero Máximo Gómez. He fought in both wars for Cuban independence, in 1868 and 1895. He sits on horseback, bravely facing the sea. This impressive statue was created by the Italian Aldo Gamba, who also made the *Fuente de las Musas* at the entrance of the Tropicana Cabaret.

214 MONUMENTO A JULIO ANTONIO MELLA

San Lázaro y L
Vedado ③

Julio Antonio Mella is the student leader who founded the first communist party in 1925. He studied law at the university of Havana until he was expelled. In 1929 he was assassinated in Mexico City. The monument to Mella holds his ashes and is located at the bottom of the university steps. In the park across San Lázaro street there are permanent black and white portraits of him.

215 MONUMENTO A ANTONIO MACEO

Malecón entre Marina
y Padre Varela,
esq Belascoain
y San Lázaro
Centro Habana ②

This sculpture pays tribute to the 'Bronze Titan' Antonio Maceo, one of the most important generals during the first war of independence in Cuba. The statue was created in 1916 by the Italian Domenico Boni, and was installed in a symbolic place, where a Spanish military fort once stood. The large white granite commemorative monument is surrounded by four figures who each incarnate one value: justice, legislation, action and ideas.

5
MUSEUMS *dedicated to*
HISTORICAL FIGURES

---

216 MUSEO LA FRAGUA MARTIANA

Príncipe no 108
esq Hospital
Centro Habana ②

Here in this forge José Martí was sentenced to forced labour for treason during his adolescent years. The Fragua Martiana first and foremost pays tribute to him. On 27 January 1953, various students met here, after Battista's coup, to commemorate the anniversary of José Martí and protest against the imprisonment of Fidel Castro. This march was subsequently called 'la Marcha de las Antorchas' and is still organized every year.

217 MEMORIAL JOSÉ MARTÍ

Plaza de la Revolución
Vedado ④

This gigantic obelisk-pyramid-tower, which stands 109 meters tall, is entirely dedicated to Cuba's national hero. At the base of the sculpture is a statue of a sitting, thinking Martí. You can find a museum about him on the ground floor. The main pillar is full of quotes by him, a good reason to visit. There are several galleries that follow his life and career and explain everything based on personal items and documents.

218 CASA-MUSEO SIMÓN BOLÍVAR

Mercaderes 156 entre
Lamparilla y Obrapía
Habana Vieja ①
+53 8613988

Take a look at the statue of Simon Bolivar on the corner of the street before entering the house. Known as the *'Liberador'* of various Latin American nations, he contributed in a decisive way to the independence of Bolivia, Columbia, Ecuador, Panama, Peru and Venezuela.

219 MUSEO ABEL SANTAMARÍA

Calle 25 no 164 apto
603 entre O y Infanta
Vedado ③
+53 7835 0891

This apartment, on the sixth floor, was a refuge for revolutionaries. Here the plans for the Moncada attacks of 26 July 1953 were hatched under Fidel Castro's supervision, with Abel and his sister Haydee Santamaría.

220 QUINTA DE LOS MOLINOS

Entre Av. Salvador
Allende, Calle Infanta
y Calle G
Vedado ③
+53 7835 0891

Once the summer residence of the Spanish governor and the residence of Máximo Goméz after the first war of independence in 1899, this museum now pays tribute to his memory.

219 MUSEO ABEL SANTAMARÍA

The 5 best places to take
SOUVENIR PHOTOS

---

221 LA LANCHITA DE REGLA Y CASABLANCA
Pier at Calle Luz
y Avenida del Puerto
Habana Vieja ⓘ

These popular little boats, which run back and forth from Havana to Regla and Casablanca have replaced the paddle steamers that were introduced at the beginning of the twentieth century. Today, they are a quaint form of transport for lots of locals going from one sector to another, along with their bicycles and all sort of belongings.

222 MALECÓN

Malecón is a magical place, for cityscapes and people. The pastels, the rundown buildings, the view of Vedado, people who want to strike up a chat, fishermen, musicians and the traffic. This is the epitome of the Cuban soul.

223 THE RAFAEL TREJO BOXING CLUB
Cuba no 815 entre
Merced y Leonor Pérez
Habana Vieja ⓘ
+53 7862 0266

Step into this open-air training facility for Cuba's local boxers. You can take magnificent photos here. This boxing club is named after Rafael Trejo, a student at the Law Faculty, who was murdered in 1930 during the protests against the dictator Machado.

224 OBISPO AND O'REILLY, PLAZA DEL CRISTO
Habana Vieja ⓘ

Daily life, colonial architecture, bars, street vendors, you name it, it's all here and you won't know where to look first. Even though you've been here hundreds of times, you'll never cease to be surprized. A stunning example of a beautiful building is bodega Potemkine in O'Reilly.

225 CASTILLO DEL MORRO
Casablanca ⓘ

This fortress was built at the end of the sixteenth century to protect Havana from attacks. Behind the lighthouse you can find a quiet spot to watch the sunset, with excellent views of the Malecón.

222 MALECÓN

The 5 most interesting
RUSSIAN MEMORIES

---

226 **SACRA CATEDRAL ORTODOXA RUSA NUESTRA SEÑORA DE KAZÁN**
Avenida del Puerto y Santa Clara
Habana Vieja ①

This monument, on the UNESCO world heritage list, was built as a symbol of the Cuban-Russian friendship. The first stone was laid in 2004. This Russian orthodox church honours the Virgin of Kazán, who is the patron saint of Mother Russia. She symbolizes victory and liberty.

227 **TABARISH**
Calle 20 no 503 entre 5ta y 7ma
Miramar ⑤
+53 7202 9188

This bar/restaurant commemorates the Cold War and memorable moments such as the reunion between Castro and Khrushchev. This venue wants to commemorate that era, but above all it celebrates the relations between the Cubans and the Russians. Go for the filete Stroganoff and the raspberry blini.

228 **COLINA LENIN**
Calle Colina entre Enlace y Rotaria
Regla

Sixty years after the death of Lenin, in 1984, a bronze sculpture of Lenin's face was carved into the cliff face by the Cuban artist Thelma Marin. Surrounding the bronze sculpture are twelve life-size white human figures, symbolizing solidarity with the October Revolution.

229 RUSSIAN EMBASSY

5ta Avenida no 6402
entre 62 y 66
Miramar ⑤

Dominating Miramar, like a sword plunged into the ground. Because of the Russian Embassy I never lose my way. It's like a compass. The building was designed by Alexander G. Rochegov and inaugurated in 1985.

230 NAZDAROVIE

Malecón no 25
entre Prado y Cárcel
Centro Habana ②
+53 7860 2947
www.nazdarovie-havana.com

This Russian restaurant Nazdarovie, meaning Cheers, has an amazing interior that boasts various Soviet-era propaganda posters and even a Lenin bust among the vodka bottles. Sit down on the balcony for a splendid view of the Malecón. The menu is full of Russian and Ukrainian favourites. Russian cuisine uses a lot of dill and parsley, ingredients that you don't find in Cuba. A farmer grows them especially for this restaurant.

229 RUSSIAN EMBASSY

The 5 most remarkable
AMERICAN LEGACIES

---

231 AMERICAN CARS

It seems like time has stood still for 50 years when you look at the traffic in Cuba. One in every five cars dates from before the Revolution. Most are American classics including models that vanished from U.S. roads.

232 ART DECO

Havana is graced with art deco buildings that date from the thirties, as well as sculptures and architectural accents. Those buildings are influenced by overseas trends where Cuban architects added tropical elements as well as African iconography.

233 TROPICANA

Calle 72 entre 41 y 45
Marianao
+53 7267 1871
www.cabaret-tropicana.com

This cabaret opened in 1939 and was known as '*Un Paraíso Bajo las Estrellas*'. This outdoor theater has been immortalized in the film based on Graham Greene's novel *Our man in Havana*. Artists who performed at Tropicana include Joséphine Baker, Cheo Feliciano, Nat King Cole, Celia Cruz, Omara Portuondo and Frank Sinatra.

234 BASEBALL

The Americans introduced Cubans to *pelota* (baseball) around 1850. Nowadays the island produces some of the finest players of this sport. The most successful team based in Havana is Industriales.

235 HOTEL NACIONAL

Calle 21 y O
Vedado ③
+53 7836 3564
*www.hotelnacional
decuba.com*

The American architectural firms Mc Kim, Mead & White and Purdy & Henderson Co were tasked with the planning and construction. The hotel has an eclectic architectural style, combining art deco, Arabic references, features of Hispanic-Moorish architecture and both neo-classical and neo-colonial elements. Their guests list impressive with names such as Ava Gardner, Winston Churchill, Ernest Hemingway and Naomi Campbell.

235 HOTEL NACIONAL

5 places to
WRITE *your postcards*
or READ *a book*

---

236 HOTEL INGLATERRA
Paseo de Martí no 416
esq San Rafael
Habana Vieja ①
+53 7860 8593
www.hotelinglaterra-cuba.com

A noisy terrace in the city center and a nice place for a drink. Alternate between your observations of daily life and some pages of the *The Selected Letters of Martha Gellhorn* after which you can do some eavesdropping on other people's conversations or mull over what you just read.

237 O2
Calle 26B no 5
entre 26 y Lindero
Nuevo Vedado ④
+53 7883 1663
www.o2habana.com

O2 may not be that easy to find but the quest is absolutely worth it. This heavenly garden terrace, is a lovely place to read a book with a drink or have a light lunch. The menu features the following quote by Eduardo Galeano: *"En las tabernas se inclubaban conspiraciones y se anuban amores prohibidos"*. Do you think this is why they chose this location? You can also consider a spa treatment or have your hair done.

238 QUINTA DE LOS MOLINOS

Entre Av. Salvador
Allende, Calle Infanta
y Calle G
Vedado ③
+53 7835 0891

Quinta de los Molinos was the residence of General Máximo Gómez and is located in the botanical gardens where you can sit down and relax for a while. This is the perfect opportunity to read a few pages of the book that you have been lugging along all days untouched. Need a reading tip? Isabel Allende's *The Island under the Sea*.

239 CAFÉ EL LUCERO

Cuba no 2 esq Aguiar
Habana Vieja ①
+53 7862 2550

This newly restored café captures both the old and new Havana with style and charm. Their welcoming terrace is the perfect place for a refreshing drink and to write your postcards. A lot of inspiration guaranteed because there's a lot to observe from various angles. The café inside has been meticulously restored and has the ability to transport you back to the past.

240 CAFÉ NERUDA

Malecón no 203
entre Manrique
y San Nicolás
Centro Habana ②
+53 7864 4159

Let the reference to the Chilean poet Pablo Neruda inspire you to write some postcards to your friends and family here. You can find a fragment of the poem *Poema 20* on one of the walls. This café, which is very popular with Habaneros, is excellent located, along the Malecón where the languorous sea breeze always has a refreshing effect.

5 of the best places to admire
STREET ART

---

241 JUAN FORMELL
Calle 46 y 21
Playa ⑤

This captivating portrait of Juan Formell is the result of a community project. Once a year the community gathers to commemorate him. Juan Formell is a Cuban bassist, composer and arranger. He is a real national hero and is best known as the director of the country's favourite band Los Van Van.

242 WRINKLES OF THE CITY
ONELIA LÓPEZ RUIZ
BY JR & JOSÉ PARLA
Calle 17 y G
Vedado ③

This is one of the few works that are still left of the marvellous mural project for the 11th Biennial. It is a portrait of Onelia López Ruiz. She wears the headscarf because of her religion. Her message to the world is about beautiful things, good things, all we need to be able is to live in peace with serenity and love.

243 BOYS
Calle 60 y Avenida 21
Playa ⑤

A charming mural of a sweet little boy. There's another one of yet another boy two blocks further. These boys could be living in this neighborhood.

244 WRINKLES OF THE CITY
RAFAEL LORENZO
Y OBDULIA MANZANO

Condesa
y Campanario
Centro Habana ②

Another mural of the 'Wrinkles of the city' project. Hurry up and see it because part of the mural is vanishing. Rafael Lorenzo was a musician so he travelled a lot, his wife never wanted to travel. When he was away from Cuba, he started to miss his wife and Cuba so much that he did not want to travel any longer.

245 LICEO ARTÍSTICO Y LITERARIO
BY ANDRÉS CARRILLO

Mercaderes
Habana Vieja ①

The mural depicts 67 human figures. Andres Carrillo used unusual techniques and mixed materials to obtain new colors and textures. The mural is located opposite the home of the Marquise de Arcos. In 1844, her house was a salon for art and culture. The wall portrays the people that visited her art room.

242 WRINKLES OF THE CITY

241 JUAN FORMELL

5

memories of Havana by

OMARA PORTUONDO

---

246 CAYO HUESO
Centro Habana ②

Cayo Hueso is a 'musical' neighborhood in the northeast of Centro Habana. The boundaries of this neighborhood are the Malecón, Calle Zanja, Calle Padre Varela and Infanta. *La comparsa de Batea* originated here as well *El Feeling* in casa de Angelito. Omara Portuondo identifies with this neighborhood. Many other musicians also lived here, such as Chano Pozo and Elena Burke. Take a walk through the neighborhood and you will encounter pure soul on every corner.

247 MALECÓN

Like many Habaneros Omara Portuondo considers the Malecón one of her favourite places. She has many good memories of this place. She would always sing a song by Farah Maria with her mother here, which went as follows: *"No te bañes en el Malecón, porque en el agua hay un tiburon"*. A choro that she likes to include in her live performances even today.

248 PARQUE TROTCHA

Calle 2 y Calzada
Vedado ③

Omara would often sit in this small garden near the Patio de la Rumba to listen to the *pregoneros*, people who offer their services or indicate what they sell in song. Omara Portuondo used to enjoy listening to them singing and would often repeat their songs.

249 GALIANO-SAN RAFAEL-TEATRO AMÉRICA

Omara also likes to visit the other side of Centro Habana. She happily remembers an unforgettable performance by *'El Barbaró del ritmo'*, the great Benny Moré in Teatro América.

250 ESTADIO PEDRO MARRERO

Avenida 41
Playa ⑤

This stadium is situated close to Salón rosado de la Tropical where Omara Portuondo's father played professional baseball. He was part of the Almendares team. Omara would often go there to see her father play.

247 MALECÓN

5 *interesting*
STATUES
WITH A LEGEND

---

251 EL CABALLERO DE PARÍS

Plaza San Francisco
de Asís
Habana Vieja ①

This person suffered a serious accident and lost his mind as a result. He spent days roaming around Habana Vieja wearing a black cape and stating to everyone that he was the 'Chevalier de Paris'. The residents and employees of restaurants would give him free food and clothes. He would give passers-by a flower. He died in 1985. A statue was installed here to commemorate him. The passers-by rub his beard for good luck.

252 JARDÍN Y STATUA DEL SAMURAI HASEKURA TSUNENAGA

Avenida del Puerto
entre Cuba
y Peña Pobre
Habana Vieja ①

Hasekura Tsunenage was the first Japanese citizen to visit Cuba in 1614. This samurai was in search of the first commercial opportunities for trade between Japan and the New World. His nickname is 'Rokuemon'. He was a war veteran who fought in the Korean wars. The bronze statue was donated by the Escuela Sendai Ikue Gukuen to celebrate the good relations between Cuba and Japan.

253 PARQUE RUMIÑAHUI

Mercaderes
y Lamparilla
Habana Vieja ⓘ

Rumiñahui was the Ecuadorian leader of the Indian resistance movement. His name means '*Ojo de Piedra*' (Eye of stone). This statue by Oswaldo Guayasamín can be found in a small park in between Lamparilla and Mercaderes in the historic city center.

254 CRISTO DE LA HABANA

Casablanca ⓘ

This sculpture was made in Italy by the Cuban artist, Jilma Madera and was inaugurated on 25 December 1958. You can see this fifteen-meter high sculpture from several places around Havana as it stands on a three-meter high base. When standing alongside the Cristo, meanwhile, you can enjoy a sweeping view of the bay of Havana.

255 LA GIRALDILLA

CASTILLO DE
LA REAL FUERZA
Plaza de Armas entre
O'Reilly y Avenida del
Puerto
Habana Vieja ⓘ
+53 7861 5010

Many people think that La Giraldilla represents Isabel de Bobadilla. She was the wife of the Spanish governor of Cuba, Hernando de Soto, who left to conquer and colonize Florida. Every day she would walk up to the top of the tower to see whether her husband was returning home.

CASA COMPAY SEGUNDO

105 PLACES
TO ENJOY CULTURE

The 5 best
M U S E U M S
to feel the Cuban soul

---

256 MUSEO NACIONAL DE LA MÚSICA

Capdevila no 1 entre
Aguiar y Habana
Habana Vieja ①
+53 8630052
www.museomusica.cult.cu

This museum for music lovers has an archive with photographs, press reviews, personal belongings, music manuscripts and instruments. Pay special attention to the music manuscript with the national hymn of Cuba by the composer himself and the piano of singer-pianist and songwriter Bola de Nieve. Currently the museum is being renovated but you can see part of the collection at Obrapía entre Bernaza y Villegas.

257 REAL FÁBRICA DE TABACOS PARTAGÁS

Industría no 520 entre
Barcelona y Dragones
Centro Habana ②
+53 7862 4604

This is one of the oldest factories. It was built by Jaime Partagás in 1845. They have 500 employees who roll Cohibas and Montecristos. During your visit you will learn more about each step in the cigar making process. In this factory they had a 'reader' who had to read the newspapers and novels out loud to entertain the cigar workers. Check visiting possibilities during works in progress.

258 CASA COMPAY SEGUNDO

Calle 22 no 103
entre 3ra y 1ra
Miramar ⑤
+53 7202 5922

Compay Segundo spent the last years of his life living in this beautiful house. He was one of the main figures of the Buena Vista Social Club. There is a permanent exhibition of photographs, personal objects, awards and some instruments such as his clarinet, the first instrument he played. With a bit of luck you'll catch Grupo Compay Segundo, led by Salvador Repilado, Compay Segundo's son, there while they rehearse.

259 FOTOTECA DE CUBA

Plaza Vieja
Mercaderes 307 entre
Muralla y Teniente Rey
Habana Vieja ①
+53 7862 2530
www.fototecadecuba.com

Created in 1986 to preserve, study and promote the country's photographic heritage and create a space for the promotion of international photography. A large collection of Cuban photographs. Also hosts fantastic temporary exhibitions. An educational role with conferences, courses and workshops. An impressive collection is the photo archive of Old Havana in the nineteenth century.

260 MUSEO DE DANZA

Línea no 205 Esq G
Vedado ③
+53 7831 2198

The history of dance told through photographs, paintings and costumes. Rooms are dedicated to the Romantic ballet, Russian ballet, National Ballet of Cuba, modern dance, Spanish dance, plastic art in relation to dance, and of course the personal collection of Alicia Alonso, Cuba's national ballet hero.

5 of the best paintings in the
MUSEO NACIONAL
DE BELLAS ARTES

Trocadero entre Zulueta y Monserrate
Habana Vieja ①
+53 7862 0140
www.bellasartes.cult.cu

261 LA GITANA TROPICAL
1929, VICTOR MANUEL
GARCÍA

The Mona Lisa of Cuba. She is every-where, on towels, posters, plates, even on shower curtains. *La Gitana Tropical* is the first classic of Cuban pictorial modernism. It has references to Gauguin and Modigliani but the painter's own creativity also shines through.

262 GUAJIROS
1938, EDUARDO ABELA

Eduardo Abela was a painter but also a comic artist. He is the creator of the character 'El Bobo' in order to protest against the Machado dictature. His mentors were Klee and Chagall.

263 UNIDAD
1938, MARIANO RODRÍGUEZ

Mariano Rodriguez, born in Havana in 1912, was an autodidact, he taught himself to paint. His moto was: *"Vivir y pintar, pintar y vivir"*. And so he did.

264 MATERNIDAD EN VERDE
1942, WIFREDO LAM

The most universal of Cuban painters. Lam integrated elements of African and Chinese origin in his work. He participated actively in the cubist and surrealist movements. Lam told the following about why he painted: "It's a way, my way, of communicating between human beings. Just one of the ways one can try to explain with full liberty. Some will do it with music, others with literature, I with painting."

265 PRIMAVERA
1940, JORGE ARCHE

A natural, poetical painting depicting a harmonious couple relaxing. A modern-day Adam and Eve, although there has been some speculation that it represents Jorge Arche and his wife, because he always pictured his wife with a flower in her hand.

MUSEO NACIONAL DE BELLAS ARTES

5 must-see
STUDIOS and GALLERIES
in Habana Vieja and Centro Habana

---

266 CASA DE LOS ARTISTAS

Oficios no 6
entre Obispo y Obrapía
Habana Vieja ⓘ

Various Cuban artists with international fame have their studios here, which you can visit and where you can see the artists at work, including Pedro Pablo Oliva, Zaida del Río and Roberto Fabelo. Contemporary art exhibitions are held downstairs.

267 CASA DE CARMEN MONTILLA

Oficios no 162
entre Amargura
y Teniente Rey
Habana Vieja ⓘ
+53 7866 8768

Carmen Montilla was a Venezuelan artist who ran this gallery until 2004 when she died. The interior courtyard is filled with sculptures and an impressive ceramic wall mural by the Cuban ceramist Alfredo Sosabravo. The work of Carmen Montilla and other Venezuelan artists is exhibited in one of the rooms.

268 GALERÍA LOS OFICIOS

Oficios no 166
entre Teniente Rey
y Amargura
Habana Vieja ⓘ
+53 7863 0497

Here you can admire the works of Nelson Dominguez, painter, sculptor and ceramist. His works have been bought by many collector and other famous people such as Robert Redford and Steven Spielberg.

269 FACTORÍA HABANA

O'Reilly no 308
entre Habana y Aguiar
Habana Vieja ①
+53 7864 9518
www.factoria
habana.com

Factoría Habana is a center for contemporary artistic and conceptual and experimental creation. The institution seeks to promote Cuba's contemporary art and wants to become a bridge between Latin American and European art. It hosts four exhibitions a year. After your visit here go to the 304 to eat some tacos and drink a piña colada.

270 STUDIO ALUAN ARGÜELLES

Salud entre Hospital
y Aramburu
Centro Habana ②
+53 7870 0784

This artist is definitely worth discovering because of his striking artworks with interesting perspectives. His work is always linked to the concept of the island and its relationship with the region around it. The topic of migration is dealt with as a whole, from the insular perspective. Here it becomes a universal given. Argüelles uses themes such as loss and the idea of seeking as starting points to develop narratives with various media.

The 5 most impressive
ARTIST'S STUDIOS
in the Vedado district and Miramar

―――――

271 GALERÍA HABANA
Línea no 460
entre E y F
Vedado ③
+53 7832 7101
www.galerihabana.com

The gallery opened in 1962 to promote Cuban art. This gallery has hosted exhibitions with work by Wifredo Lam, René Portocarrero, Mariano Rodriguez and Amelia Peláez. Nowadays they show the work of young creators such as Roberto Diago and maestros like Manuel Mendive. Nationally and internationally recognized artists.

272 GALERÍA COLLAGE HABANA
Calle D no 10
entre 1ra y 3ra
Vedado ③
+53 8333826

This gallery used to be at San Rafael but it moved to Vedado. The gallery works with a catalogue of talented artists including lots of young creators who represent the newest aesthetic trends. Drop in, there's always something interesting going on.

273 GALERÍA ARTIS 718

Calle 7ma esq 18
Miramar ⑤
+53 7204 7106

Galería Artis 718 opened in September 2014 as a result of the efforts made by the Fondo Cubano de Bienes Culturales. Here you can see exhibitions of paintings, drawings, photographs, sculptures, installations, art videos and performances. Important names such as Ernesto Fernandez and José Manuel Fors are associated with this gallery.

274 GALERÍA VILLA MANUELA

Calle H no 406
entre 17 y 19
Vedado ③
+53 7832 2391
www.galeriavilla manuela.com

This art gallery of the UNEAC, the Union of Writers and Artists of Cuba, is as a cultural complex that was founded as the result of an exchange with the Deputation of Barcelona. Villa Manuela is an interdisciplinary contemporary art space that exhibits and promotes the work of its members. It also has a supply store and a book store.

275 ESPACIO AGLUTINADOR

Calle 6 no 602
entre 25 y 27
Vedado ③
+53 7830 2147
www.espacio aglutinador.com

Espacio Aglutinador is the oldest independent art space in Cuba. It was created in 1994 by artists Sandra Ceballos and Ezequiel Suarez. This gallery shows and promotes the work of Cuban artists of all sectors, alive or dead, known or unknown, promoted or almost forgotten, modest or pedantic. All are welcome.

5 graves you should leave a flower on in
CEMENTERIO COLÓN

Calle 12 y Zapata
Vedado ④
+53 7832 1050

276 ALEJO CARPENTIER

Cemetery Colón was founded in 1871 and is dedicated to the man who discovered the island. Covering an area of 56 acres, the cemetery is considered the largest in America. One of the graves you should visit is that of Alejo Carpentier, a Cuban writer and musicologist.

277 LA MILAGROSA

Thousands of Habaneros visit the tomb of Amelia Goyri, La Milagrosa, in hopes that their wishes mostly related to motherhood will come true. Amelia Goyri died giving birth to her first child which didn't survive either. When the grave was exhumed, bodies were found intact and the baby, who had been buried at her feet, was found nestled in her arms. This legendary motherlove caused people to attribute special powers to her.

278 MÁXIMO GÓMEZ

This Dominican military hero was recruited by José Martí himself and played a crucial role in Cuba's independence. Gómez died in 1905. His tombstone is a bronze obelisk with a small, round portrait on it.

279 RUBÉN GONZÁLEZ, IBRAHIM FERRER, JUAN FORMELL

Walk past the graves of musicians of the Buena Vista Social Club, including the pianist Rubén González and the singer Ibrahim Ferrer. Since 2014, Juan Formell, the bandleader of Los Van Van is also buried here.

280 CATALINA LASA AND JUAN PEDRO BARÓ

Cuba's most famous twentieth-century lovers are buried in this art deco mausoleum. Catalina died in Paris in 1930. Baró commissioned a tombstone from the French glass artist René Lalique.

CEMENTERIO COLÓN

5 of the best
CULTURAL CENTERS

---

281 TALLER DE SERIGRAFÍA RENÉ PORTOCARRERO

Cuba no 513 entre
Teniente Rey y Muralla
Habana Vieja ①
+53 7862 3276

It displays and sells paintings and prints of the most promising artists in Havana. You can also see the artists at work. Named after René Portocarrero, a major Cuban painter, whose subjects relate to the Afro-Cuban tradition but in a poetic manner. His work is exhibited in the Museo de Bellas Artes.

282 FÁBRICA DE ARTE CUBANO

Calle 26 esq 11
Vedado ③
+53 7838 2260
www.fac.cu

The place to go in Havana at the moment. F.A.C is an artistic project led by X-Alfonso to support and promote art in a large sense and to a large audience. He attempted and succeed in giving the Cubans a meeting place with all the artistic manifestations under one roof. Worth queueing for.

283 CENTRO DE DESARROLLO DE LAS ARTES VISUALES

San Ignacio entre
Teniente Rey y Muralla
Habana Vieja ①
+53 7862 2611

In the casa Carmen Montilla is a ceramic wall by Alfredo Sosabravo. Here you can see an intriguing sculpture by the same artist in the courtyard. Art education classes are given on the second floor. There is an art gallery on the top floor.

284 INSTITUTO CUBANO DEL ARTE E INDUSTRIA CINEMATOGRÁFICOS

Calle 23 no 1155
entre 10 y 12
Vedado ③
+53 7552864
www.cubacine.cult.cu

The ICAIC was established a few days after the victory of the Revolution. This to show the importance and great valor of artistic culture. They are the principal producers of movies and documentaries and also responsible for the Cinemateca de Cuba, the film archives, the film festival and the promotion and distribution of Cuban cinema.

285 CENTRO DE ARTE CONTEMPORÁNEO WIFREDO LAM

San Ignacio no 22
esq Empedrado
Habana Vieja ①
www.wlam.cult.cu

This eighteenth-century house used to be a post office, a bank, a school. Now it is one of the most important art galleries, named after one of Cuba's most important modern painters, Wifredo Lam. This state-run cultural complex was set up for the study, research and promotion of contemporary visual arts.

282 FÁBRICA DE ARTE CUBANO

281 TALLER DE SERIGRAFÍA RENÉ PORTOCARRERO

5 of the most intriguing
LITERARY PLACES

---

286 CASA MUSEO JOSÉ LEZAMA LIMA

Trocadero no 162 entre
Industria y Consulado
Centro Habana ②
+53 7863 4161
www.cnpc.cult.cu

This is where the poet, writer and art critic José Lezama Lima lived from 1929 until 1976. His furniture, family portraits, his library: everything has been kept unchanged. It feels as if you are visiting him and that you are waiting for him to put in an appearance. Here Lezama wrote his most famous work *Paradiso*.

287 FUNDACIÓN ALEJO CARPENTIER

Empedrado no 215
entre Cuba y San
Ignacio
Habana Vieja ①
+53 7861 5506
*www.fundacion
carpentier.cult.cu*

The Fundación can be found in the Casa del Conde de la Reunión. Alejo Carpentier wrote his novel *El siglo de las luces* here. A part of the house is dedicated to his memory. His early works are displayed here, and his raincoat is still thrown over his old deskchair. The rest of the house is used as a cultural center.

288 CASA NATAL JOSÉ MARTÍ

Leonor Perez no 314
entre Egido y Picota
Habana Vieja ①
+53 7861 3778

Birth house of national hero and poet José Martí, born on 28 January 1853. It is recently renovated, and has a permanent exhibition of the events that formed Martí's personal and political life.

289 CENTRO CULTURAL DULCE MARÍA LOYNAZ

Calle 19 y E
Vedado ③
+53 7835 2732
www.centroloynaz.cult.cu

Dulce María Loynaz was a Cuban poet and writer. In 1992, she received the Spanish Premio Cervantes. Lots of major writers such as Frederico García Lorca visited her in Cuba. She lived in this house in Vedado until she died in 1997. It is now a cultural literary center. You can still visit three rooms, which have been preserved in their original state.

290 STATUE OF CECILIA VALDÉS

Plazuela del Ángel,
Compostela no 1
esq Cuarteles
Habana Vieja ①

Cecilia Valdés is a character in a novel by Cirilio Villaverde, the Balzac of Cuba. His novel is set in the 1830s colonial Havana, and it is considered important for its literary quality and its insight into the interaction of classes and races. The novel was adapted for the silver screen by Humberto Solas.

286 CASA MUSEO JOSÉ LEZAMA LIMA

The 5 best
HEMINGWAY-ANDO

---

291 FINCA VIGÍA
Follow Carretera
Central from Havana
for 12,5 km
San Francisco de Paula
+53 7891 0809
www.hemingway
cuba.com

This is the house where Hemingway lived the longest, from 1939 till 1960. He wrote several books here including *The old man and the sea*. Drink a cocktail Vigía (guarapo, pineapple and lemon) before leaving. Gabriel García Marquez once said that when a writer has several residences his real home is where his books are. Hemingway had a library of more than 9000 books so it's safe to say that if we believe in Marquez's adage Hemingway was happy in this place.

292 AMBOS MUNDOS
Obispo no 153
esq Mercaderes
Habana Vieja ①
+53 7860 9530
www.hotelambos
mundos-cuba.com

Hemingway stayed in this hotel from 1932 till 1939. He always stayed in room 511. You can still visit it, the room hasn't changed since he lived there. You can see his glasses, typewriter, writing table and other memorabilia. Martha Gellhorn, Hemingway's third wife, refused to live here with him and that's how they ended up at Finca Vigía. The first chapters of *For Whom the Bell Tolls* were written here.

291 FINCA VIGÍA

293 COJÍMAR

293 COJÍMAR

Cojímar is the fishing village where Hemingway kept his boat, Pilar. The figure of Santiago, the old fisherman, the main character of *The Old man and the Sea*, was inspired by Hemingway's real life fishing partner in Cojímar, Gregorio Fuentes. When Hemingway died, everyone in the village collected metal pieces from propellers, chain links and anchors to use as material for a bronze bust of Hemingway.

294 LA BODEGUITA DEL MEDIO

Empedrado no 207
entre Cuba
y San Ignacio
Habana Vieja ⓘ
+53 7571375

This is the place where Hemingway drank his mojito. Here he wrote the following sentence on butcher's paper: 'My mojito in La Bodeguita del Medio, my daiquiri in La Floridita'. Past visitors such as Salvador Allende, Fidel Castro, Nat King Cole, Harry Belafonte have all left their autographs on the wall.

295 CAFÉ BOHEMIA

Plaza Vieja
San Ignacio 364
Habana Vieja ⓘ
+53 7860 3722
*www.havana
bohemia.com*

Time has come to taste an 'Old man and the sea'-sandwich at Café Bohemia. Read a chapter of the book *Adios Hemingway* by the Cuban writer Leonardo Padura. The protagonist of the story is Mario Conde, who would prefer to be a writer instead of doing detective work. The story unfolds in the fifties, the period in which Hemingway faced two of his greatest fears: his inability to work and his death. Padura tries to understand Hemingway throughout this murder mystery.

5 places for
DANCE and
'SALSA EN VIVO'

---

296 CAFÉ CANTANTE MI HABANA
Avenida Paseo esq 39
Plaza de la Revolución
Vedado ③
+53 7878 4273

You can find Café Cantante in the cellar of the Teatro Nacional. Great groups play here with a good audio and large mixed audience. As Amaray, the singer of Manolito Simonet y su Trabuco, would say: *"Esta caliente"*.

297 CASA DE LA MÚSICA GALIANO
Galiano entre
Neptuno y Concordía
Centro Habana ②
+53 7860 8296

You'll find the best Cuban salsa in this spacious old theater. There are two concerts a day, one at 5pm and one at 9pm but the actual concerts usually only start at 7 and 11pm respectively. Here you can catch Pupy y Los que Son, Son, they play here twice a week. Don't miss it. Check what's on at *www.lapapeleta.cult.cu*.

298 CASA DE LA MÚSICA MIRAMAR
Calle 20 esq 35
Mirama ⑤
+53 7204 0447

An institution on the Havana salsa scene. Here Alexander Abreu and his Havana D'Primera perform on Tuesdays and Thursdays when they are not touring. The best of the best, of the best. Don't hesitate, slip on your dancing shoes and off you go. Fiesta. El Diablo Tun-Tun, a piano bar, is in the same building.

299 JARDINES DEL 1830

Malecón 1252 esq 20
Vedado ③
+53 7838 3091

Best time to come to this place is on Sundays. Salsa concerts are organized in the exquisite gardens of this colonial mansion facing the sea. Always check who's playing before going, to be sure of a good crowd and good music.

300 SALÓN ROSADO DE LA TROPICAL

Avenida 41 esq 46
Playa ⑤
+53 7203 5322

All-time favorite. Also best on Sunday, but the same rule applies here. Always check who's playing. Try to catch Maykel Blanco y su Salsa Mayor, Los Van Van, Issac Delgado. Nice atmosphere, lots of energy and very 'real' Cuba. Also check El Sauce at Avenida 9na entre 120 y 130, Playa, another great outdoor concert venue. You will definitely want to return.

---

301 JAZZ CAFÉ
GALERÍAS DE PASEO
Calle 1ra y Paseo
Vedado ③
+53 7838 3302

The best jazz players perform here, in the Jazz Café. Try to catch jazz pianist Roberto Fonseca. Your entrance fee also covers your drinks so you can eat here before the concert starts. Feel the good vibes and have a nice evening.

302 LA ZORRA Y EL CUERVO
Calle 23 entre N y O
Vedado ③
+53 7833 2402

This is one of Cuba's most famous jazz bars. You enter through a red telephone box on the popular Calle 23. There's an intimate and nice atmosphere present at this excellent location. It's rather difficult to find out who is performing, just go and ask.

303 CAFÉ JAZZ MIRAMAR
5ta Avenida no 9401
esq 94
Miramar ⑤

Café Jazz Miramar is where Cuba's best musicians jam and improvize. The modern venue has a stage that's practically in the center of the room, resulting in amazing acoustics. This is a non-smoking bar, unlike lots of others.

304 CAFÉ TEATRO BERTOLT BRECHT

Calle 13 esq I
Vedado ③
+5378329359

El Café Brecht is also called 'No le digas a nadie' (don't tell anyone). This contemporary place hosts gigs with different kinds of music. On Tuesdays Interactivo plays here. Save the date in your agenda please because you cannot miss the opportunity to see them live. A funky place with a hipster Cuban crowd.

305 KARL MARX THEATER

Avenida 1ra
entre 8 y 10
Miramar ⑤
+5372030801

The best venue for world class musicians. Benny Moré played here, as well as Silvio Rodríguez and Pablo Milanés. The font used for the name of the venue is also worth a photograph. Even if you're not going to a concert, don't forget to snap a photo.

305 **KARL MARX THEATER**

5 places to enjoy
TRADITIONAL and TROVA MUSIC

---

306 **SALÓN 1930 'COMPAY SEGUNDO'**
HOTEL NACIONAL
Calle O esq 21
Vedado ③
+53 7836 3564
www.hotelnacional
decuba.com

This venue is in the Grand Hotel Naciónal. Start your night with a cocktail, as you look at the sea and enjoy the airy breeze that wafts in from the Malecón. Afterwards, go and see the concert. One Saturday you'll find the Orquesta Aragon on stage, the other Saturday it will be Grupo Compay Segundo. Never mind the groups of tourists. Just enjoy the excellent traditional music.

307 **GATO TUERTO**
Calle O entre 17 y 19
Vedado ③
+53 7838 2696

After the concert we just mentioned, you'll find it's still quite early. Since it's 11 pm, why not head to the Gato Tuerto to listen to some fabulous bolero singers. Where Omara Portuondo once sang, you can now hear the voices of Ivette Cepeda and Osdalgia.

308 CLUB BARBARAM PEPITO'S BAR

Calle 26 entre Avenida Zoológico y 47
Nuevo Vedado ④
+53 7881 1808

This place was decorated and inspired by the animation movie *Vampiros en la Habana*. The name of the bar refers to Pepito, the main character of the movie. Pepito represents 'el Cubano': a good friend, in love, familiar, brave, with a good sense of rhythm and a musician. The Vampisol costume hangs here. Vampisol allowed vampires to withstand the rays of the sun. An interesting place where you can enjoy some of the best Cuban Nueva Trova performances.

309 TRADICIONALES DE LOS 50

SOCIEDAD ROSALIA DE CASTRO
Egido no 504 entre Monte y Dragones
Habana Vieja ①
+53 5270 5271
www.tradicionalesde los50musicacubana.com

Tradicionales de los 50 is a project that started 15 years ago and which pays tribute to the Golden Era of Cuban Music in the fifties. Names like Celia Cruz and Benny Moré are part of that prestigious musical heritage. A two-hour show starts every night at 9.30 pm.

310 EL JELENGUE DE AREITO OR PATIO DE LA EGREM

San Miguel no 410
Entre Campanario y Lealtad
Centro Habana ②
+53 7862 0673

A tiny venue with a great variety of musical genres: on Mondays and Tuesdays there is traditional music on the menu, Wednesday is all about trova, Thursday it's time for some vitrola, rumba on Fridays and Sundays rumba and bolero on Saturday, el Carnaval del Amor. You can also buy music and posters here.

306 **SALÓN 1930 'COMPAY SEGUNDO'**

5 places
YOU WOULDN'T EXPECT
to find in Havana

---

311 JOHN LENNON PARK
Calle 15, 17 y 6, 8
Vedado ③

Against all expectations, people in Cuba also like the Beatles. This park owes its name to the sculpture of John Lennon. It was unveiled by Castro himself in 2000. Obviously the bronze sculpture was wearing glasses but they were frequently stolen. As a result, a security guard is now responsible for the sculpture.

312 CEMENTERIO CHINO
Calle 26 y Zapata
entre 28 y 33
Nuevo Vedado ④
+53 7830 4517

At one time Cuba had the biggest Chinese community in the Americas. So it will come as no surprise that they decided to build a Chinese cemetery in 1892. This eternal resting place is subdivided into four quadrants, which represent heaven, earth, the world of the living and the world of the dead.

313 CASA VICTOR HUGO
O'Reilly no 311
entre Aguiar y Habana
Habana Vieja ①
+53 7866 7590

This cultural center hosts French language classes, screens French films and also has a library with French books. In addition to this, there is also an exhibition space and a space dedicated to Victor Hugo.

314 JARDÍN DIANA DE GALES
Baratillo
esq Carpinetti
Habana Vieja ①

Take a look at the beautiful inscription above the garden entrance and step into this tiny zen oasis. Artworks by Alfredo Sosabravo and Juan Quintanilla and an engraved plaque from Princess Diana's home of Althorp, which was donated by the British embassy, also grace the garden.

315 MUSEO NAPOLEÓNICO
San Miguel no 1159
esq Ronda
Vedado ③
+53 7879 1412

This museum is dedicated to the huge Napoleon Bonaparte collection of sugar magnate Julio Lobo and the politician Orestes Ferrara. The most interesting attractions during your visit are the sketches of Voltaire, a recreation of Napoleon's study and bedroom and one of the seven death masques that were cast two days after Napoleon's death by his personal physician.

313 CASA VICTOR HUGO

5

HOUSES TO VISIT

with eyes wide open

---

316 CASA DE LA OBRA PÍA
**Obrapía no 158
esq Mercaderes
Habana Vieja** ①

This prestigious casa is a stunning example of baroque architecture in Havana. The ground floor is all about Alejo Carpentier. Here you can admire the VW Beetle he used when working as a cultural attaché at the Cuban embassy in Paris. The house also has a stunning collection of eighteenth-century objects, paintings and furniture.

317 CASA DE GUAYASAMÍN
**Obrapía entre Oficios
y Mercaderes
Habana Vieja** ①
+53 7861 3843

The contemporary Ecuadorian artist Oswaldo Guayasamín died in 1999. You can see a large number of his works in his private home. The screen prints he made are especially impressive. Guayasamin's art is a sight to behold as is the location itself, a magnificent colonial palace.

318 CASA DE AFRICA

Obrapía no 157
entre Mercaderes
y San Ignacio
Habana Vieja ⓘ
+53 7861 5798

This colonial house represents African culture. The collections from 27 African countries are based on the collection of Fernando Ortiz, the first anthropologist to coin the term Afro-Cuban. It also relies on Fidel Castro's collection, which consists almost entirely of items he received in lieu of thanks for assistance. The institution also features religious objects that are used in Afro-Cuban religion.

319 CASA DE BENITO JUÁREZ

Obrapía no 116
esq Mercaderes
Habana Vieja ⓘ
+53 7861 8166

This eighteenth-century colonial house, which aims to disseminate Mexican culture, was established in 1988. The museum is named after the president of Mexico who visited Havana twice. The galleries focus on the artisan aspect of Mexican culture, with its different techniques and materials. Pay special attention to the precious Alfonso Reyes library, which has over six thousand publications on the history, art and traditions of Mexico.

320 CASA DEL AGUA LA TINAJA

Obispo no 111 entre
Oficios y Mercaderes
Habana Vieja ⓘ

No mojitos, no rum, no beer. Here you can only buy filtered water to commemorate the 'water houses', on which Habaneros relied for their water supply. The eccentric owner pretends that 'his' water is better than bottled water. This shop is a real 'cultural' experience.

5 very
SPECIAL MUSEUMS
in Havana

---

321 MUSEO DE LA FARMACIA HABANERA

Teniente Rey y
Compostela
Habana Vieja ①
+53 7866 7554

This museum narrates the history of pharmacies in Havana and the evolution of pharmaceutical science in Cuba. The interior is incredibly beautiful and a real treat for aficionados of bottles and vials. Besides medicine, they also sell lotions and creams which they prepare themselves.

322 MUSEO POSTAL CUBANO

Rancho Boyeros
entre 19 de Mayo
y 20 de Mayo
Vedado ③
+53 7870 5581

This museum gives you another perspective on two centuries of Cuban history through stamps. The old writing materials and precious documents including the account books of the first administrator dating from 1765 are equally interesting.

323 MUSEO DEL MINISTERIO DEL INTERIOR

Calle 14 entre 3ra y 5ta
Miramar ⑤
+53 7202 1240

This museum hosts intriguing exhibitions that link to CIA espionage. It documents several assassination attempts on Fidel Castro including the poison capsules which the CIA is said to have used to try and kill him.

324 MUSEO DE LA CAMPAÑA DE ALFABETIZACIÓN

Avenida 29E esq 76
Marianao
+53 7260 8054

This museum documents the literacy campaign that started on 1 January 1960. More than 120.000 people spread out across the country to teach the illiterate to write and read. To get to the museum you must walk through the entrance of Ciudad Libertad school. Take a look at the schoolgirl and schoolboy carved out of stone in the pillar to the right of the entrance.

325 MUSEO NACIONAL DEL DEPORTE

Rancho Boyeros
y Bruzón
Vedado ③
+53 7814696

The permanent collection of this museum includes medals, trophies, sporting clothes, equipment and photographs. Special objects include Che Guevara's rifle, the chess set, chairs and clock belonging to Capablanca, the boxer Kid Chocolate's dressing gown and gloves.

324 MUSEO DE LA CAMPAÑA DE ALFABETIZACIÓN

The
BIG 5
of Centro Habana and Habana Vieja

---

326 **CAPITOLIO**
**Prado entre San José
y Dragones
Centro Habana** ②
+53 7863 7861

Completed in 1929 under Machado and inspired by the Capitol in Washington. This building has a diamond in its floor, which acts as the zero point for all distances within Cuba. As of 1959 the Capitolio was transformed into the Academy of Science and the Ministry of Science and Technology.

327 **CATEDRAL DE
SAN CRISTÓBAL**
**Plaza de la Catedral
Empedrado y
San Ignacio
Habana Vieja** ①

In 1748, construction started on this church, which was commissioned by the Jesuits. This baroque church was made a cathedral when the old Parroquial Mayor crumbled. As of 1796, it was called San Cristóbal cathedral, because people thought that the relics of Christopher Columbus were here until 1898, when they were transferred to the cathedral of Seville. There is a statue dedicated to the great explorer inside.

328 PLAZA VIEJA
**Teniente Rey,
Muralla, San Ignacio,
Mercaderes
Habana Vieja** ①

The Plaza Vieja which we all know today as the beautifully restored square which spans four centuries of architecture was once used for Havana's largest slave market. When the Plaza de Armas was invaded by the military, the Plaza Vieja was used as a replacement. It was called Plaza Nueva at the time. In the seventeenth and eighteenth centuries, this was considered a prestigious square.

329 MUSEO DE BELLAS ARTES
**Trocadero entre
Zulueta y Monserrate
Centro Habana** ②
+53 7862 0140

The most impressive museum in all of Habana. Discover its enormous Cuban art collection, which comprizes about 4300 paintings, 12.800 drawings and 285 sculptures. You can see works here by Wifredo Lam, Raúl Martinez, Amelia Pélaez and René Portocarrero. A real revelation and a fantastic discovery. The universal section exhibits items from 500 BC to the present.

330 MUSEO DE LA CIUDAD DE LA HABANA
PALACIO DE LOS
CAPITANES GENERALES
**Tacón 1 entre Obispo
y O'Reilly
Habana Vieja** ①
+53 7861 5779

The Spanish governors resided in this baroque building until 1898. Under the Republic it was used as the presidential palace. Nowadays this palace is home to the Museo de la Ciudad. It has a very complete collection, which tells the city's story right up until the revolution. The museum also exhibits a copy of José Martí's *Versos Sencillos* containing the poem that everyone knows: *La Guantanamera*.

5 of the most
SACRED STATUES
and PLACES

---

331 LA VIRGEN DEL CAMINO
Crossing of Calzada
de Luyano, San Miguel
del Padrón y Carretera
Central
San Miguel del Padron

This sculpture was designed by the
Cuban artist Rita Longa. The Virgen del
Camino holds 'la rosa de los Vientos' in
one hand, which guides travellers. She
opens your roads, as the Cubans always
remind us. Traditionally visitors leave a
coin in the fountain.

332 IGLESIA NUESTRA SEÑORA DE LA MERCED
Cuba no 806
esq Merced y Paula
Habana Vieja ①
+53 7863 8873

This church is beautifully decorated
with religious frescos and old paintings.
There are links with Afro-Cuban
religion. Nuestra Señora de la Merced
symbolizes fertility and purity, which
are the characteristics of the orisha
Obbatalá in the Yoruba cult. On 24
September the people come here to
venerate her, all dressed in white.

333 IGLESIA SANTA RITA
5ta Avenida y 26
Miramar ⑤

This modern church was designed by
architect Victor Morales. Santa Rita is
the patron saint of hopeless causes, the
advocate of the impossible. Many
venerate her because they hope she will
put an end to their unsolved problems.

334 **GRAN SYNAGOGA BETH SHALOM**
Calle I no 251
entre 13 y 15
Vedado ③

In 1981, a large part of this synagogue, which was built in 1952, was sold to the Cuban state, which used it for the Bertolt Brecht cultural center. Beth Shalom is the headquarters of the Cuban-Jewish community. The synagogue also has a Jewish library.

335 **CASA DE LOS ARABES**
Oficios no 16
esq Obispo y Obrapía
Habana Vieja ①
+53 7862 0082

The Friday prayers are organized here in this Casa de los Arabes, an Arabic cultural center and ethnographic museum. The Casa de los Arabes belonged to a rich Arab, who lived here in the forties. It was inspired by Andalusian architectural designs.

331 LA VIRGEN DEL CAMINO

5 also
INTERESTING PLACES
in Havana

---

336 NAME PLATE OF FREDRIKA BREMER
Oficios entre Obispo y Obrapía
Habana Vieja ①

The Swedish author and feminist Fredrika Bremer (1801-1865) wrote the epistolary novel *The Homes of the New World*, in which she regales her sister Agathe with tales of her visit to Havana in February 1851. She adored the green, orange and yellow colors of the houses in Habana Vieja. Fredrika Bremer is considered the Swedish Jane Austen.

337 TERESA DE CALCUTA
Plaza Francisco de Asís
Habana Vieja ①

In the rear section of the convent of San Francisco de Asís you can see commemorative portrait/statue of Mother Theresa. It was created by José Villa Soberón. Walk through San Francisco de Asís square, to the extreme left of Caballero de Paris to enter the park. It's also a nice place to catch your breath.

338 CASA DE LA POESÍA

Muralla no 63 entre
Oficios y Inquisidor
Habana Vieja ①
+53 7862 1801

This cultural center is tasked with the promotion and dissemination of poetry through direct contacts with authors and poets. It has a 'Sala Abierta' which focuses on the work of young Cubans. Artisan creations, photos, ceramics and paintings are exhibited here. In another space, the 'Sala transitoria', the casa focuses on iconography and various projects of publishers.

339 MUSEO DE ARTE COLONIAL

Plaza de la Catedral
San Ignacio no 61
entre Empedrado
y O'Reilly
Habana Vieja ①

This museum exhibits seventeenth-, eighteenth- and nineteenth-century furniture, as well as stained glass and porcelain collections and many other carefully preserved objects. The house was built in 1720 and belonged to Don Luis Chacón, a citizen of Havana who was appointed Military Governor of Cuba three times.

340 MUSEO DE ARTES DECORATIVAS

Calle 17 no 502
entre D y E
Vedado ③
+53 7832 0924
+53 7830 9848

This residence belonged to José Gomez Mena and his family. The family was forced to flee after the revolution, bricking up their cellar where they had hidden all their treasures. Their collection of more than 3000 item is now exhibited here in ten galleries. The Limoges porcelain, Lalique's art deco creations, a desk that once belonged to Marie-Antoinette. These are just a few of the items on display here.

5 remembrances to
AMELIA PELÁEZ
throughout Havana-city

---

341 LAS FRUTAS CUBANAS
HOTEL HABANA LIBRE, 1957
Calle L entre 23 y 25
Vedado ③

Amelia Peláez is a ceramic artist and painter and is considered one of Cuba's leading visual artists. You can see several works by her throughout Havana. The best known is her vast mural of blue, white and glass tiles adorning the Habana Libre.

342 FLORAS AMARILLAS
MUSEO DE BELLAS ARTES
Trocadero entre
Zulueta y Monserrate
Centro Habana ②
+53 7862 0140

Amelia Peláez made still-lifes popular again by mixing in Cuban and cubist motives. Floras amarillas is a still-life from Amelia Peláez's later period and dates from 1964. It marks a return to simpler compositions.

343 CASA
MUSEO AMELIA PELÁEZ
Estrada Palma no 261
entre Juan Bruno
Zayas y Consejal Veiga
La Vibora

This house was built in 1912. In 1915, the Peláez family moved in. Over time, it gradually became a meeting place for artists and writers. Today you can visit her house and studio. Several of her works are on display, as well as the objects that inspired her to create them.

344 GALERÍA DE ARTE AMELIA PELÁEZ
Calle Cortina
Arroyo Naranjo

An art gallery that exhibits the work of Amelia Peláez. You can also follow ceramics workshops here. You drive past the art gallery on the way to the mausoleo Celia Sanchez. Not that far from the lake in Parque Lenin.

345 MURAL
MINISTERIO DEL INTERIOR
Plaza de la Revolución
Vedado ③

In the fifties, Amelia Peláez designed a mural for the Edificio del Tribunal de Cuentas, which now houses the Ministry of the Interior. It is entirely made of beautiful azulejos.

341 LAS FRUTAS CUBANAS

5 of the most popular
MUSIC STYLES

346 DANZÓN

The *danzón* originated from Haiti and then arrived in France in the eighteenth century. In Cuba it is mentioned for the first time around 1870, through African and European immigrants. A lot of Cuban music originates in *danzón*. It was very popular with the slaves and the *campesinos*, but also with other social classes, across the entire spectrum.

347 SON

The cradle of *son* is in Santiago de Cuba. Itinerant workers of the sugar cane plantations in Oriente brought *son* to Havana. The Spanish immigrants introduced the guitar, while African slaves added the rhythms and percussion. After slavery was abolished, African folk songs were added to the Spanish folk songs, creating *son* in the twenties. The musicians mainly use light instruments such as the tres, claves, maracas, bongo and the bas.

348 CHANGUI

Changui originated in the city of Baracoa, in the province of Guantanamo. *Changui* is the predecessor of *son* and a combination of Spanish influences and African rhythms. The tres and the bongo are the key elements, the marimbula is used to produce the bass tones.

349 GUAGUANCO

Guaguanco is a type of *rumba* which combines percussion, singing and dance. It all started with the ordinary *guaguanco* singer, who would perform and sing stories and anecdotes and also comment upon political events and scandals. Over time, percussion and dance were added.

350 RUMBA

Rumba are African rhythms, which originated in slavery. There are three types of rhythms in Cuba: *yambu*, *columbia* and *guaguanco*. *Cajones* were replaced in the twentieth century with *tumbadoras* (congas). Successful rumba bands include Los Papines, Los Muñequitos de Matanzas and Yoruba Andabo.

The 5 best
FESTIVALS

─────────────

351 FERIA INTERNACIONAL DEL LIBRO

This annual international book fair always takes place around mid-February in La Cabaña. The feria attracts large numbers of people. The atmosphere is pleasant. A wide range of books are available, especially translated literature. Several activities, linked to books and music, are scheduled. After the books are presented in Havana, a smaller version of the fair travels to the other provinces. Every year the feria invites a guest country.

352 FIESTA DEL TAMBOR
www.fiestadeltambor. cult.cu

Congas, claves and maracas. El Teatro Mella is all ablaz during the annual Tambor days in March. A week of many activities and concerts that are all in some way related to percussion with countless master classes, an international percussion competition, activities which promote the support and conservation of percussion culture with African influences, performances and so on.

353 FESTIVAL DE BOLEROS DE ORO

This festival for romantic souls is organized by the UNEAC every year in June. Often the spotlight is on a singer, Daniel Santos in 2016. As is the case for other festivals, everything is organized in several venues, such as Teatro America, Huron Azul of UNEAC and Centro Hispanoamericano de Cultura.

354 FESTIVAL DEL NUEVO CINÉ LATINOAMERICANO
*www.habana
filmfestival.com*

Every year, around 15 December, film is the main attraction in Havana. There are several competitions, based on an official selection and other criteria. The festival was organized for the first time in 1979. ICAIC is in charge of organizing it. The first prize is the 'Gran Premio Coral. *Fresa y chocolate* won a prize several years ago.

355 FESTIVAL DE JAZZ
www.jazzfestival2016.com

This festival partly overlaps with the Film Festival. The city dances to the sounds of jazz, with excellent performances all over Havana. Major names, upcoming artists and above all, a lot of quality and innovation.

5

MORE

if you're up for it

---

356 ASGER JORN MURALS
OFICINA DEL HISTORIADOR
Calle 23 y L
Vedado ③

Wifredo Lam met Danish painter Asger Jorn in Italy and invited him to Havana. During their visit to the Historic Archive, Jorn expressed his desire to paint murals on the eleven empty walls, on the theme of the origin of the Cuban revolution from his neo-expressionist perspective.

357 MUSEO ANTROPOLÓ-GICO MONTANÉ
FACULTAD DE BIOLOGIA-UNIVERSIDAD DE LA HABANA
Calle 25 no 455
Vedado ③
+53 7879 3488
fbio.uh.cu/mmontane.php

The collection of the Montané anthropological museum has an exceptional collection of pre-Columbian art. One of the most important pieces is the wooden sculpture of the Idolo de tabacco from Baracoa. The Taíno Indians used it for grinding tobacco leaves during their ceremonies. The museum opened in 1903.

358 GABINETE Y MUSEO DE ARQUEOLOGÍA
Tacón no 12 entre
Plaza de la Catedral
y Plaza de Armas
Habana Vieja ①
+53 7861 4469

This office was founded to conduct research into the old houses in the historic city center. The conclusions have given rise to various recovery and restoration projects of dwellings, market places and the foundations of the city. Don't miss the Taíno art collection.

359 MUSEO DE HISTORIA NATURAL FELIPE POEY

FACULTAD DE BIOLOGIA-
UNIVERSIDAD DE LA
HABANA
Calle 25 no 455
Vedado ③
+53 7879 3488

This zoological laboratory was established in 1874 and founded by the scientist Felipe Poey. Many personal items and his books are exhibited here as well as his scientific collections of Cuban fauna and flora. Stuffed sharks, squirrels and iguanas are just a fraction of what is on display here. The whale suspended from the ceiling is the museum's crowning glory.

360 CENTRO HISPANO-AMERICANO DE CULTURA

Malecón no 17 entre
Prado y Capdevila
Habana Vieja ①
+53 7860 6282

The centro Hispano-Americano is inspired by the traditions of the Institución Cubana de Cultura, which was founded by Fernando Ortiz in 1926. The main purpose of this centro is the reading of the Spanish-language classics and a reflection on various topics such as identity, social science and art.

359 MUSEO DE HISTORIA NATURAL FELIPE POEY

PELOTA

30 THINGS TO DO WITH CHILDREN

―――――

The 5 best
ACTIVITIES
WITH CHILDREN

---

361 CÁMARA OSCURA

Plaza Vieja
entre Teniente Rey
y Mercaderes
Habana Vieja ⓘ
+53 7866 4461

Located on the roof of an eclectic early twentieth-century house, this is the perfect place to enjoy a spectacular 360-degree view of all of Old Havana through a telescopic lens, the *cámara oscura*, in a dark room. Twin of the Tavira Tower in Cádiz, Spain, this *cámera oscura* was the first in America. There are only five others in the world: two in England, two in Spain and one in Portugal. The *cámara oscura* was invented by Leonardo da Vinci. An unforgettable experience.

362 EL PLANETARIO

Plaza Vieja
Mercaderes no 311 entre
Teniente Rey y Muralla
Habana Vieja ⓘ
+53 7864 9165

The planetarium is an interactive cultural center that provides a fascinating look into the origins and structure of the universe. The impressive telescope can capture up to 6500 stars which are displayed around a large sphere. Enjoy your trip to the stars.

361 **CÁMARA OSCURA**

362 **EL PLANETARIO**

363 **COCHE PRESIDENCIAL MAMBÍ**

363 COCHE PRESIDENCIAL MAMBÍ

Oficios entre
Teniente Rey y Muralla
to the side of
Palacio de Gobierno
Habana Vieja ①

A train carriage, which was built in the U.S.A. in 1900 and brought to Cuba in 1912. It was used as a presidential car and is a veritable palace on wheels with an elegant dining room and louvered wooden windows. Because of its comfort and exclusivity, the train carriage was very popular with candidates and Cuban presidents during elections in the first half of the twentieth century.

364 MUSEO DE NAIPES

Muralla 101
esq Mercaderes
Habana Vieja ①
+53 7860 1534

This playing cards museum is situated in the oldest building of Plaza Vieja. It boasts a collection of more than 2000 cards. There are also postcards and posters, all related to playing cards. Workshops are organized here as well as magic shows.

365 MAQUETA DE LA HABANA

Calle 28 no 113
entre 1ra y 3ra
Miramar ⑤
+53 7202 7303

This modern pavilion contains an enormous model with a scale of 1:1000 and depicts the whole city. Measuring 22 by 8 meters, this model is one of the tallest in the world. Its scale allows the observer to identify each street, place and monument. Buildings and houses are painted in various colors depending on the period in which they are built.

The 5 most popular
CUBAN STREET GAMES

366 **4 ESQUINAS**

Two of the most frequently played games on the island's streets, namely *4 esquinas* and *juego del taco*, originated in *pelota* (baseball). *4 Esquinas* or 4 corners is a form of *pelota* played on the street using four corners of a street intersection and involves four players. A smaller bat, a smaller ball and no gloves are used as the distance is much shorter. *4 Esquinas* comes in different variations.

367 **JUEGO DEL TACÓ**

You draw a square on a wall to indicate the strike zone. Instead of a ball you usually use a small piece of rubber which is hurled forcefully against the wall in an attempt to strike out the batter. The batter uses an improvized bat and gets a run if he can get past the defense in the safe zone. The winning team is the first team to reach the agreed number of runs.

368 LA CHIVICHANA

Of all the 'toys' this the most Cuban of artefacts. It's fun to sit down on the rolling board or in the rolling car but it's even more fun to make it together with friends or family.

369 JUEGO DE LA PAÑOLETA

A game which involves different teams. A battle to 'steal' the *pañoleta* (scarf) in the center of the playground, or from someone who holds it in his hand.
One of several members of the group are encouraged to grab the *pañoleta* without being caught by the opponent.

370 JUEGO DE YAQUIS

You need twelve jacks, one bouncing ball and two players. You have to throw your jacks in front of you. After that you throw your ball in the air, pick up one jack, then catch the ball after it bounced once. You have to continue picking up jacks one at a time. After collecting all your jacks you continue the game by picking up two jacks at a time. The favourite game of Cuban children at school during playtime.

366 PELOTA

5 lovely
SWIMMING POOLS
and BEACHES

---

371 CLUB ALMENDARES

Calle 49C esq 28A
Kohly
+53 7204 4990

This club is close to the Parque Almendares. It has a nice pool with various eating and recreation facilities. The entry fee is 10 cuc that covers foods and drinks for an amount of 8 cuc.

372 HOTEL RIVIERA

Paseo y Malecón
Vedado ③
+53 7836 4051

The sixteen storey Hotel Riviera has an outdoor pool with diving boards, a three level one. It's the only pool in Havana with that option. The pool has barely changed since it opened in the late fifties.

373 SAN ANTONIO DE LOS BAÑOS

Here you can enjoy a boat trip along the Rio Ariguanabo. Embark at the boat dock near Hotel Las Yagrumas. A motor boat will take you on an 8-km spin. You can also rent rowing boats. While you're there, you should also consider visiting the Museo del Humor, esq Calle 60, with its fun selection of cartoons. San Antonio de los Baños has also an arty side. Silvio Rodriguez was born here, and Gabriel Garcia Marquez helped establish the International Cinema and TV school.

374 **PLAYA JIBACOA**

This undiscovered paradise has small and splendid beaches. Lots of Cubans come here. You can enjoy a nice time at the beach but there are also lots of interesting things to do in the surrounding area, especially with children, like taking the electric Hershey train.

375 **PLAYA GUANABO**

Playa Guanabo is a charming beach with palm trees. It is visited by mostly Cubans. Few crowds and no big hotels. Quinta avenida, the main street, has a lot cafés and shops.

375 GUANABO

The 5 must-do
ESCAPES
WITH CHILDREN

---

376 CUEVA DEL INDIO
PARQUE NACIONAL VIÑALES
Carretera a San Vicente
+53 8796280

This underground cave in the Valle de San Vicente will delight children with its spooky bat-ridden stalactites and stalagmites. The main thrill is a boat ride on an underground river that emerges into the open air. Horseback rides are also offered.

377 PARQUE LENIN
Calle 100 y Cortina
de la Presa
Arroyo Naranjo
+53 7644 2721

This park, which covers a surface area of 8 km², has several attractions. One of the main attractions is the Parque Mariposa, a Chinese-designed theme park that was built in 2007. This is Havana's best attraction for young children. There are twenty different rides including a rollercoaster, bumper cars and a 42-m high ferris wheel. You can see all sorts of fish, crabs, turtles and even a couple of crocodiles in the aquarium.

378 EXPOCUBA

Carretera del Rocío
km 3
Calabazar

Expocuba is a permanent exhibition of Cuban industry, science, technology, sports and culture. It has 34 pavilions including booths that display the crafts, products, music and dance of each of Cuba's provinces.

379 PARQUE ALMENDARES

Below the bridge on
Calle 23
Nuevo Vedado ④

A magical and enchanting urban forest in the city with a recreational area for children with pony rides and a playground. Lots of sites mention boating on the river but the boats are no longer available for renting. In the amphitheater, families can enjoy puppet shows and magic shows.

380 PARQUE ISLA DE COCO

5ta Avenida y 112
Miramar ⑤

A Chinese-designed theme park. Besides the mechanical attractions such as rollercoasters and flying swings there are also simple games that children appreciate like pillow fighting. Balloons, clowns, magicians, ice creams, it's easy to see why lots of Cuban families like to come here during weekends.

The 5 best places
for crocodiles, dolphins,
CIRCUS *and* THEATER

---

381 CRIADERO DE COCODRILOS

Boca de Guamá

+53 4591 5562

This crocodile breeding farm was set up as conservation project in order to save the then-endangered Cuban crocodile and U.S. crocodile from extinction. The farm itself is not designed to welcome visitors but the show pen has a small swamp with pads around it. It contains a few crocs who are left alone. You can also visit during one of the twice-weekly feeding sessions.

382 ACUARIO NACIONAL DE CUBA

Avenida 3ra y 62
Miramar ⑤

+53 7202 5871

www.acuarionacional.cu

Crowds come here to see the sea lion and dolphin shows. The Acuario is also a scientific center specializing in marine research and environmental protection awareness and promotion. Visit the biodiversity exhibition, a *marine grotto* (coastal cave) and a tropical island area with an 186.000-gallon reservoir with 30 different specimens of marine tortoises including the Caguama turtle, shell turtle and green tortoise.

383 CIRQUE NACIONAL DE CUBA

5ta Avenida y Calle 112
Playa ⑤
+53 7206 5609
www.circonacional
decuba.cu

Carpa Trompoloco (Trompoloco circus tent) is the headquarters of the Cuban National Circus. Circus performances are on Saturday and Sunday. The rest of the week the building hosts a varied programme with shadow plays, theater performances, concerts and other events. Some of the attractions of the National circus are jugglers, the Strongman Trio, balancing objects, fire-eaters, magic and illusionism and clowns.

384 TEATRO GUIÑOL

Calle M entre 17 y 19
Vedado ③
+53 7832 6262

Leading children's theater and puppetry company. They perform on this stage as well as in public areas. If there's no show while you are visiting Havana also check the schedule of El Arca at Avenida del Puerto y Obrapía, Habana Vieja, +5378648953. There is a puppet museum with delightful puppetry shows.

385 SALA DE TEATRO DE LA ORDEN TERCERA

Officios y Muralla
Habana Vieja ①
+53 7860 7699

This is the home base of the prestigious children's theater La Colmenita. The aim is to strengthen the cultural ties with underprivileged neighborhoods of Havana and other provinces by performances of classics plays by Shakespeare and Tirso de Molina.

5 more
INTERESTING PLACES
to visit with children

---

386 PARQUE DEL AGRIMENSOR
Egido y Arsenal
Habana Vieja ①

In this park you can admire restored locomotives. These used to be kept in sugar warehouses. Fortunately, the decision was made to restore them and gather them in this place, near the station. One of the locomotives, with number 1112 made by Baldwig, built in 1878, was used in the documentary about José Martí, *el Ojo del Canario*, by the director Fernando Pérez.

387 BARRIO CHINO
Zanja y Dragones
Centro Habana ②

The presence of the Chinese in Cuba dates from the nineteenth century. They were brought here as farm workers for the sugar cane plantations. Later a wave of Chinese arrived from California, who opened businesses here. Thanks to them, mangos were introduced to Cuba. They cultivated them in small plots. The center of this neighborhood is Cuchillo de Zanja, which looks almost folkloric thanks to the typically Chinese decoration.

388 EL BANCO DE CHOPIN
Plaza Francisco de Asís
Habana Vieja ①

The sculpture of the Polish composer Chopin by artist Adam Myjak was inaugurated in 2010. This bench is a meeting place for many people and usually also a location for a photo shoot for the portfolio of fifteen-year old girls. When girls turn fifteen in Cuba this is celebrated with a lavish party, called 'los quince'. A portfolio is made in different outfits. The girls look splendid and show their album off to everyone.

389 MUSEO NACIONAL DE HISTORIA NATURAL
Plaza de Armas
Obispo no 61
esq Oficios
Habana Vieja ①
+53 7863 9370
www.mnhnc.inf.cu

The origin of life and earth and its evolution are represented in this museum with several objects. The gallery with stuffed birds, reptiles and mammals, with sounds of nature, is definitely fun to see. The fifteen-million-year-old petrified turtle is one of the main draws of this museum.

390 MUSEO DE LOS BOMBEROS
Zulueta no 257 entre
Neptuno y Animas
Centro Habana ②
+53 7863 4826

The firehouse, which opened in 1909 and was used until 2008, now is home to a nice museum which tells the story of the Cuban firemen. Their uniforms, their equipment, water tanks and fire engines are all on display here in this museum.

CASA ALINA

20 PLACES
TO SLEEP

The 5 most charming
INDEPENDENT APARTMENTS

391 BOHEMIA BOUTIQUE APARTMENTS
Plaza Vieja
Habana Vieja ①
+53 5403 1568
www.havana
bohemia.com

Gorgeous and beautifully decorated apartments. There are three apartments available, the Bohemia Red, the Bohemia Blue and the Bohemia White. Enter through the cool patio of Café Bohemia where breakfast is served. They also have one room to rent, called Bohemia Estancia.

392 SUITE HAVANA
Lamparilla no 62
entre Mercaderes
y San Ignacio
Habana Vieja ①
+53 5829 6524
www.suitehavana.com

Suite Havana consists in an elegant two-bedroom apartment in a restored colonial house in one of the nicest streets of the historic center. A quality loft style décor will make your stay more than pleasant. The jacuzzi will offer you a perfect way to relax.

393 CASA CONCORDIA
Concordia no 151 ap 8
esq San Nicolas
Centro Habana ②
+53 5413 4724
www.casaconcordia.net

Beautifully designed and spacious three-bedroom apartment. Spanish colonial interiors with cheerful, arty accents.

394 CASA ARTE HABANA

San Miguel no 101
apt 7 entre Industria
y Amistad
Centro Habana ②
www.casa-arte-
habana.com

Casa Arte Habana is a perfect example of Spanish colonial architecture. This four bedroom apartment has the most splendid view of the Capitolio. People of the neighborhood tell Fidel Castro lived in one of them while studying for his law degree. A warm welcome is given by Maria Elena. You'll want to spend the rest of your life in this gigantic, stunning apartment.

395 TROPICANA PENTHOUSE

Galiano no 60 entre
San Lázaro y Trocadero
Centro Habana ②
+53 5413 4724
www.tropicana
penthouse.com

This luxurious penthouse is precious for its huge rooftop and breath-taking 360-degree views of Havana and the ocean. The bedrooms with a touch of green and red are spacious and really comfortable. It's nice staying here.

394 CASA ARTE HABANA

The 5 best
BOUTIQUE HOSTELS

396 CAÑAVERAL HOUSE

Calle 39A no 4402
entre 44 y 46
Playa ⑤
+53 7206 5338

An outstanding private home with a
pool. This Spanish style hacienda with
large arches and doorways was built in
1949. It underwent a major renovation
in 2014, retaining the splendid
architecture of large living rooms
and spacious bedrooms. The interior
is a sophisticated and tasteful mix of
artefacts of the Cuban Golden Age with
European and modern style furniture.

397 HOSTAL GUANABO

Calle 480
entre 1ra y 3ra
Guanabo
+53 7799 0004
www.hostal
deguanabo.com

Terrific five-bedroom seafront villa,
which is a 20-meter walk from the
beach of Guanabo, 30 km to the east
of Havana. Pool and jacuzzi. All the
rooms are comfortable and beautifully
decorated and they all have beach-
related names like sol, mar, brisa, arena,
espuma. You will definitely enjoy a
marvelous stay here.

398 CASA ESCORIAL

Plaza Vieja
Mercaderes no 315 apt 3
entre Muralla
y Teniente Rey
Habana Vieja ⓘ
+53 5278 6148

Large apartment with a panoramic view of Plaza Vieja above Café Escorial. You'll wake up to the aroma of the freshly made coffee downstairs. A cook will come prepare your large breakfast.

399 LA ROSA DE ORTEGA

Patrocinio no 252
esq Juan Bruno Zayas
La Vibora
+53 7641 4329
www.larosadeortega.com

A marvellous place to stay and relax, on the city's second highest hill, La Loma del Mazo. This hill boasts impressive views of the ancient villa of San Cristóbal de la Havana. Beautiful and comfortable rooms, a pool and magnificent garden where you will be served breakfast. Julia and Silvio, your hosts, are always ready to assist you when needed. The perfect place to rest and get to know a lovely, tourist-free neighborhood of Havana. A location to keep in mind.

400 VITRALES

Habana no 106 entre
Cuarteles y Chacón
Habana Vieja ⓘ
+53 7866 2607
www.cvitrales.com

Hospitable, attractive and reliable B&B with nine bedrooms in a republican building in the historic center of Havana. High quality accommodation with personalized services. Chill out on the rooftop terrace.

The 5 best places to sleep in a
CASA PARTICULAR

401 CASA ALINA

Calle E no 562
entre 23 y 25
Vedado ③
+53 5258 7544

A beautiful three-bedroom house. All rooms have a private shower and toilet. Enjoy a wonderful breakfast with a lot of fresh fruit in the nicely decorated living room where you are surrounded by books, a piano and art. End your breakfast with a *cafecito* in the rocking chairs on the front patio.

402 CASA AMADA MALECÓN

Calzada no 55
entre M y N
Vedado ③
+53 5296 7768
www.casaamada.net

Comfortable and basic clean rooms with a private bathroom, fridge and air conditioning. Delicious and copious breakfast in a cosy space with a view of the Malecón. An extremely friendly service in a top-notch location. Enjoy some artist spotting over breakfast.

403 CASA ALTA

San Ignacio no 412
apto 2 entre Sol
y Muralla
Habana Vieja ①
+53 5341 4873
www.casaaltahabana.com

This newly-renovated, family-owned *casa particular* has six bedrooms and is located near Plaza Vieja. Enjoy stunning views of Havana from the rooftop terrace. Spacious, modern yet charming rooms that feel like home. A delicious and copious Cuban breakfast is served.

404 CASA SEÑORA TANIA

Calle 29 entre B y C
Vedado ③
+53 7835 3652

Two large, comfortable rooms under the roof of a magnificent house, opposite Starbien, one of the finest paladars in the Vedado. Don't forget to admire the lovely details in the balcony. Excellent breakfast with the best *guava batido* you will find in Havana. If you don't know where to spend your evening, ask because here they always know where you should go.

405 STUDIO GISEL

Calle 22 no 116
entre 1ra y 3ra
Miramar ⑤
+53 5267 9427

If you want to act like a local or like someone who's really living here, you can rent this practical, very well equipped, air conditioned studio that is part of a house but has a separate entrance. Breakfast is served in the house. An excellent option.

401 CASA ALINA

The 5 most special or luxurious
HOTELS and HOUSES

406 HOTEL TERRAL

Malecón esq Lealtad
Centro Habana ②
+53 7860 2100

The recently renovated Hotel Terral has fourteen rooms with a fantastic view of the Malecón and ocean. The rooms are all decorated in a chic, minimalist style. The inviting lobby will definitely catch your eye as you drive past on the Malecón.

407 CONDE DE VILLANUEVA

Mercaders no 202
esq Lamparilla
Habana Vieja ①
+53 7862 9293

An intimate hotel with nine rooms in an eighteenth-century palace. The room names refer to well-known Cuban cigars such as 'Perla de Llevada'. They also have a Casa del Habano. The perfect accommodation for cigar aficionados.

408 RESIDENCIA MARIBY

Calle 11 no 513
entre D y E
Vedado ③
+53 5370 5559
www.mariby.com

A large luxurious townhouse, with colonial-style interiors and Louis XV furniture. They offer a wide range of services, such as a chef who will prepare your dinner or a relaxing massage. The covered section of the terrace with bamboo rocking chairs will make you dream of luxuriating here forever with your favourite book.

409 HAVANA CASA BLANCA

Morro-Cabaña Park
House no 29
Casablanca ⓘ
+53 5294 5397
www.havana
casablanca.com

Havana Casa Blanca is an elegant, restored nineteenth-century house, which was once owned by Fulgencio Batista. It is rented as one house for maximum five guests. The savage garden with fruit trees and tropical birds as well as the exceptional view of the bay of Havana make this a delicious place to unwind after a day in the bustling center.

410 HOTEL RAQUEL

Amargura no 103
esq San Ignacio
Habana Vieja ⓘ
+53 7860 8280

A stunning art nouveau gem, inspired by Jewish culture. The rooms on the first floor all have biblical names such as Abraham and Isaac. On the second floor they are named after Jewish heroines such as Hannah and Esther. The hotel itself is named after the biblical figure, Rachel, who died in Canaan while giving birth to her son Benjamin. If you don't choose to stay here, do pop in to admire the roof terrace and its breathtaking view.

CINE YARA

45 ACTIVITIES
FOR WEEKENDS

———

The 5 must-visit places in
CIENFUEGOS

---

411 PASEO DEL PRADO BENNY MORÉ

Cienfuegos was founded in 1819 by immigrants from Bordeaux and the American French colonies. Its wide boulevards, neoclassical flamboyance and eclectic architecture epitomize the Gallic approach to urban planning. Listen to the voice of Benny Moré singing: *"Cienfuegos es la ciudad que màs me gusta a mí"*. With that in mind stroll down the animated Prado, and take a souvenir picture with the bronze statue of Moré.

412 TEATRO TOMÁS TERRY AND JARDINES DE LA UNEAC

Avenida 56 no 270
entre Calle 27 y 29
+53 4351 3361

This magnificent eclectic building with both French and Italian influences was built between 1887 and 1889 to honour the Venezuelan industrialist Tomás Terry who invested a large amount of money in this project. Artists such as Caruso and Sarah Bernhardt performed here. After this architectural visit, go and have some fun in Cienfuegos's best venue, Jardines de la UNEAC (Calle 25 entre Avenida 54 y 56), with an outdoor leafy patio that hosts Afro-Cuban peñas, trova, bolero, son and top local bands.

413 CEMENTERIO LA REINA

Esq Avenida 50
y Calle 7
+53 4352 1589

The city's oldest cemetery with many graves of Spanish soldiers who died in the War of Independence. The bodies are interred above the ground in the walls due to the high groundwater levels. A highlight here is the marble statue of the *Bella Durmiente* at the grave of a young woman who died of a broken heart in 1907.

414 GUANAROCA LAGOON

The road from Cienfuegos to Rancho Luna crosses a narrow branch of the Bahía of Cienfuegos. To the east of the bridge lies the Laguna Guanaraco, a lovely place to spot flamingos, pelicans and other wildlife. You can take a guided nature walk here. Afterwards rowboats take the visitors out into the Laguna. Flamingos come and go and are a spectacular sight when they are there. Go early in the morning.

415 EL NICHO WATERFALLS

Take a trip to the enchanting cascading waterfalls, pools and caves in the green Sierra del Escambray mountains, where you will be surrounded by pure nature.

The 5 best places in
ALAMAR

---

416 EL CHANCHULLERO

Calle 5ta G no 16204
entre 162 y 162D
Zona 6
www.el-chanchullero.com

A second Chanchullero opened in Alamar, a coastal suburban neighborhood on the outskirts of Havana. *"Todo lo que sucede, sucede por una razón"* ("everything that happens, happens for a reason"), those are the words of the young self-taught managers who opened these magical bars. Good food and good prices in a really, really nice place, more than worth the trip.

417 THE GARDEN AND GALLERY OF AFFECTION

HÉCTOR GALLO

Building 11c
Micro x

Typewriters and sewing machines, primitive TVs, ancient swords, mystical animal bones, children's shoes and ballerina slippers, curious unfinished sculptures and canes. Including personal sayings written on pieces of metal or dry leaves. This is the art installation or alternative museum in the front garden of poet and artist Hector Gallo. When Gallo moved from Vedado to Alamar, he began to collect abandoned items on the streets because nothing is useless. It just depends on how you look at things.

418 ORGANIPÓNICO VIVERO ALAMAR
PARQUE HANOI

Zona 6
Habana del Este
+53 7763 0531
www.farmcuba.org

Vivero Alamar is an organic farm that was founded in 1997 by Miguel Salcines and three others, to feed the neighborhood during the Special Period. Now it's completely sustainable and organic and employs 160 people, selling 90% of its produce to locals with only 10% going to restaurants. You can buy fresh produce, sugarcane juice, jams and jellies here. If you call ahead, they can prepare you a nice lunch too.

419 HOME STUDIO CIRENAICA MOREIRA

Calle Real no 183
entre Carmen
y Montaña
Cojímar

Cirenaica Moreira's works speak about being a woman, mother, daughter, lover and citizen of a country like Cuba, in Havana in the late nineties and the early years of the new century. Her studio is located in the fishing village of Cojímar. The house is perched on a sun-drenched inlet that flows into a nearby harbor. Ernest Hemingway once docked his boat near the artist's now-crumbling patio.

420 EL ANFITEATRO DE ALAMAR

Zona 1
Calle 3ra
Habana del Este

Alamar is the birthplace of Cuban rap which has its roots in the economic crisis and collapse of Cuba's ally, the Soviet Union. Alamar is a town with a population of more than 250.000 inhabitants where many rap groups were formed such as Papa Humbertico and Orishas. Each year in August, a hip hop festival is held at the Anfiteatro.

The 5 best places to explore
CUBAN NATURE

---

421 LAS TERRAZAS

Built as a model rural community and located on the edges of a lake, this mountain village is an ecotourism center. You have to pay an entry fee at the tollbooth to enter the village and you will be required to listen to a short history of the village, there's no escaping it. Las Terrazas is known for various things: the open artist's studios, the Polo Montañez museum, Hotel Moka, and the Cafetal Buenavista, a beautifully restored coffee plantation. When leaving Las Terrazas, stop for a delicious cappuccino at Café de Maria where they excel at latte art. Look into your coffee to discover Che looking up at you.

422 SOROA

Sixteen kilometers southwest of Las Terrazas, you will find Soroa, a tiny village with an orchid garden with a collection of more than 700 species. You can enjoy treatments, with water from the fresh mineral springs. Spend some time in the romantic pool, *la poza del Amor*.

423 VALLE DE VIÑALES

A sleepy, pretty village where you can chill. You'll run into a green landscape with mogote mountains, underground caves and lakes about 160 km southwest of Havana. The tobacco plantations here supply many of Havana's cigar factories. Perfect for hiking, rock climbing and horseback riding. Or maybe you prefer to unwind at the swimming pool overlooking the serene valley (Hotel Los Jazmines or Hotel La Ermita).

424 CUEVA DE LOS PECES

Carretera entre Playa
Larga y Playa Girón
Península de Zapata
Matanzas

A natural aquarium that is 61 meters deep or a flooded cave with tropical multi-colored fish. Walk along a short shaded trail to the saltwater pool and dive in or you can also snorkel from the beach. Exploring the darker parts of the cenote is possible. There's an on-site diving shop where you can rent tanks and snorkelling gear. One of the most tranquil spots on the Península.

425 PARQUE NACIONAL GUANAHACABIBES

Visitor Center
La Bajada
+53 4875 0366

This is one of the largest protected areas in the country, established by UNESCO in 1987. It has a variety of habitats including coral reefs, beaches, mangroves, scrublands, and evergreen forest. Guanahacabibes is home to more than 170 species of birds and dozens of reptiles and mammal species. The second largest breeding population of green turtles in the country nests on its beaches.

The 5 most
SPIRITUAL ESCAPES

---

426 SANTUARIO DE SAN LÁZARO

Carretera de San
Antonio de los Baños
El Rincón
Santiago de las Vegas

This small church is the final destination of one of the most important pilgrimages in Cuba every 17th of December. The church is a venerated shrine of the Christian Saint Lazarus, who was known for his ministrations to lepers and the poor. This saint, who is identified as Babalú-ayé in the Afro-Cuban religion Santeria, has a reputation for extra-ordinary miracles that help people with health problems. People offer prayers to the image of the saint, lighting candles and placing flowers before him.

427 IGLESIA DE SANTA MARIA DEL ROSARIO

Calle 24 entre 31 y 33
Santa María del
Rosario, Cotorro
+53 7682 2183

This is a charming colonial village and home to this church which was built between 1760 and 1766. The church was given its name by Obispo Espada, 'the cathedral of the fields of Cuba'. It has a baroque altar of amazing beauty, only comparable with the altar of the Church of Remedios. The famous writer Alejo Carpentier got married here in 1940.

428 MUSEO MUNICIPAL DE GUANABACOA

Martí no 108 entre Valenzuela y Quintín Bandera
Guanabacoa
+53 7797 9117

This historical museum tells the story of Guanabacoa's development and the evolution of Afro-Cuban culture through one of the most complete ethnographic collections. An important item to see is 'la Tribuna del Liceo Artistico y Literario de Guanabacoa' from where José Martí pronounced his first speech in 1879.

429 CENTRO CULTURAL RECREATIVO DE LOS ORISHAS

Martí no 175 entre Lamas y Cruz Verde
Guanabacoa
+53 7794 7878

While you're in the heart of Havana's Santería you can eat or/and drink something in the garden of this cool bar-restaurant, where you are surrounded by colorful Afro-Cuban sculptures. There's a good selection of food and live rumba music.

430 MUSEO MUNICIPAL DE REGLA

Martí no 158 entre Facciolo y La Piedra
Regla
+53 7797 6989

Regla is a Santería center. Note the tiny shrines outside many houses. Calle Calixto García has many examples. Many *babalawos* (Santería priests) live here and will happily dispense advice for a fee. Try Eberardo Marero (Ñico Lopez no 60 entre Coyola y Camilo Cienfuegos). The Museo Municipal tells the story of the town's Santería associations.

The 5 best places for
DAZZLING ROMANCE

431 PALACIO DE LOS MATRIMONIOS
Paseo de Martí
esq Ánimas
Centro Habana ②

Sit on a bench watching Cuban couples getting married. Each weekend from 11 am. Stunning neo-renaissance architecture with a *salon de baile* (a ballroom) that takes up the entire upper floor. Sometimes it is hard to get in. It's worth just watching happy people, dressed up colorful, taking photos.

432 CINÉ YARA
Calle L esq 23
Vedado ③
+53 7832 9430

A romantic date for many Cubans. Share some *palomitas de maíz* (popcorn) while watching a film. Afterwards eat some ice cream together at Coppelia in front of the Yara. It is the most popular cinema in the city and is considered the cornerstone of Cuban modernist architecture.

433 DOS GARDENIAS
EL SALÓN DEL BOLERO
Avenida 7ma esq 26
Miramar ⑤
+53 7204 2353

A romantic moment, singing along with the *boleristas*. The name of the place refers to the famous romantic song *Dos Gardenias* and pays tribute to the singer Isolina Carrillo. Haila, 'La Diva del Son', sings a specific repertoire of ballads here on Wednesdays.

434 HEARTS OF FUSTERLANDIA
ESTUDIO JOSÉ FUSTER
Calle 226 esq 3A
Jaimanitas

Count charming hearts of the mosaic installation in the magic kingdom of José Fuster. Fuster is an exponent of illumination and joy. The work of this skilled painter, draughtsman, sculptor and ceramics artist has a conceptual and stylistic unity. More than eighty neighbors allowed Fuster to use their homes as his canvas to create an artistic wonderland. He is called the Picasso of Cuba.

435 LA GUARIDA
Concordia no 418 entre
Gervasio y Escobar
Centro Habana ②
+53 7866 9047
www.laguarida.com

Climb up the dramatic marble staircase to the top floor for a romantic dinner among old film paraphernalia where the light is dimmed. Don't go away without having a pineapple-ice cream dessert after your tuna steak with a sugarcane glaze.

434 HEARTS OF FUSTERLANDIA

The 5 most interesting
WORKSHOPS
to follow

---

436 **LA CASA DEL SON**

Empedrado no 411
entre Aguacate
y Compostela
Habana Vieja ①
+53 7861 6179
www.bailarencuba.com

Dance classes, Cuban percussion as well as Spanish language lessons. Almost everything is possible in the Casa del son, which was especially created for visitors who want to learn, enjoy and improve their skills in Cuban traditional dances. There are six salons with ideal conditions. No fixed schedules but courses are planned based on your own plans and schedules during your stay. There's no excuse.

437 **CONJUNTO FOLKLÓRICO NACIONAL DE CUBA**

Calle 4 no 103 entre
Calzada y 5ta
Vedado ③
+53 7830 3060
www.folkcuba.cult.cu

If you want to learn Cuban rhythms, enquire about the possibilities of percussion or dance classes. Some of the leading dancers of the National Folklore group of Cuba will teach you the secrets of Cuba folk dances with their African and Hispanic roots as well as the magic sounds produced by Cuban percussion instruments. There are several levels to learn mambo, son, chachacha, rumba, santería dances, conga, batá and more.

438 ARTECHEF

Calle 3ra y A
Vedado ③
*www.havana
xperience.com*

Artechef is a restaurant and project that is managed by la Federación de Asociaciones Culinarias de la República de Cuba. For the foodies and cooking lovers this is the place to be. You can learn to cook Cuban *comida criolla* taught by chefs.

439 TALLER EDITORIAL EDICIONES DE VIGÍA

Plaza de la Vigía
esq Calle 91
Matanzas
+53 4524 4845

This publishing cooperative produces and showcases handmade books. Each cover and also the pages within the book are works of art. Vigía uses repurposed materials such as paper from the local butcher, yarn, fabric, leaves, dried flowers, tin foil to produce a limited number of volumes. A maximum of two hundred copies of each book is published. Visitors are welcome in the Matanzas workshop.

440 TALLER DE GRÁFICA CONTEMPORÁNEA

EDIFICIO
MARÍANO RODRÍGUEZ
Avenida Central
y Final no 28
Villa Panamericana
Habana del Este
+53 7766 0826

The famous Cuban artist Nelson Dominguez, along with his artist children Liang and Li, opened their contemporary graphics workshop to all creators. Group seminars and private classes are available for beginners and anyone who's interested in learning more about the printmaking process. You are invited to come visit, learn, produce and share.

5 of the nicest
ACTIVITIES
for a SATURDAY

---

441 PROYECTO COMUNITARIO LA MURALEANDO

Aguilera esq 9 de Abril
Luyanó/Lawton
www.muraleando.org

In 2001, two local artists, Manuel Diaz Baldrich and Ernesto Quirch Paz, began teaching art workshops in the community school. When their classes conflicted with the computer program, they moved their workshops into the streets and the seeds of Muraleando were sown. Check it out.

442 KCHO ESTUDIO ROMERILLO

7ma esq 120
Playa ⑤
+53 7883 1663
www.kchostudio.com

This contemporary art complex, opened by the renowned artist Alexis Leiva Machado alias Kcho, contains a library, a theater, experimental workshops and galleries that intend to show the works of leading artists worldwide.

443 ESTADIO LATINO-AMERICANO

Zequera no 312
Cerro ④

This stadium is the largest in the country with 55.000 seats. It's the home of Industriales, Havana's baseball team, which is also called Los Azules or Los Leones.

444 SALÓN DE BELLEZA CALLE A

Calle A no 112 apto 2
entre 1ra y 3ra
Miramar ⑤
+53 7202 1033

It's Saturday and you want to sparkle like all the other beautiful Cuban ladies. Start by enjoying a heavenly massage. Then go for a mani-pedi, choose from one of a million colors and eavesdrop. It's like you're a real Habanera. Once your nails are done, go get your hair styled. You'll leave completely zen, and looking your best. Professional, helpful and extremely friendly staff, all with magic hands and fingers.

445 ROMA RENT BIKE

Compostela no 255
entre O'Reilly y Obispo
Habana Vieja ①
+53 5501 3562
www.rentbikehavana.com

Another way to experience the city is to explore it by bike. There's a lot of traffic with its 'own' rules and different types of vehicles, all driving at different speeds. Do take the challenge, you will experience Havana with all your senses.

441 PROYECTO COMUNITARIO LA MURALEANDO

The 5 best
CINEMAS

446 CINE CHAPLIN

Calle 23 no 1157
entre 10 y 12
Vedado ③
+53 7831 1101

This is the Cinemateca of Havana. An art house cinema that screens Cuban and international movies. The venue has 1200 seats and the lobby features a poster gallery of great Cuban classic films. In 2015, this was one of the first cinemas in Cuba to be fitted with digital projection facilities.

447 LA RAMPA

Calle 23 no 111
entre O y P
Vedado ③
+53 7878 6146

La Rampa was initially a bowling alley but now it is used as a cinema. They also have a film archive. This cinema screens films throughout the day. Various festivals are organized at La Rampa, including the European film festival.

448 CINE RIVIERA

Calle 23 no 507
entre G y H
Vedado ③
+53 7832 9564

In the evening, the white letters on top of this blue cinema turn a bright blue. It screens a wide range of films, including action movies from North America, the UK and Cuba. Also lots of Spanish-language movies from Latin America. And it hosts good live concerts of pop, rock and rap groups.

449 CINE ACAPULCO

Avenida 26
entre 35 y 37
Nuevo Vedado ④
+53 7830 9564

The Aacapulco was a luxury cinema that opened in 1958. It had a beautiful modern interior. Now a little run down, it still screens premieres of Cuban movies and a variety of other films.

450 CINE INFANTA

Infanta entre
Neptuno y San Miguel
Centro Habana ②
+53 7878 9323

This multiplex has four modern cinemas. An important venue during the international film festival in December. In Cuba going to the cinema is a real experience, because Cubans express their emotions during the film. They laugh, are frightened, tell the characters what they should do, reflect on what's not done. In short, they comment on every bit of the film without being disruptive. It's like interactive cinema, but more fun.

448 CINE RIVIERA

The 5 most interesting
REVOLUTIONARY ESCAPES

451 MONUMENTO ERNESTO CHE GUEVARA

Plaza de la Revolución
Santa Clara

In this museum, entirely dedicated to Che Guevara, you can learn more about his life, through photos and documents. Afterwards you can also visit the mausoleum where an eternal flame burns near the body of Che and other soldiers. This is probably the only place in Cuba where all is silent. A large statue of Che stands atop the mausoleum, making this an elegant tribute to this guerrilla fighter.

452 MONUMENTO A LA TOMA DEL TREN BLINDADO

Calle Independencia
Santa Clara

Che Guevara and his three hundred men conquered a city that was defended by 3000 men. The day after, Che delivered another crushing blow to Battista, by destroying the railway on which the train with Battista's troops would ride. The armoured train derailed, allowing Che to take control. Four of the derailed train cars have been preserved, to commemorate this astonishing victory, some of which are now used as a museum.

453 MUSEO DE PLAYA GIRÓN

Playa Girón

Museo Girón opened in 1981 to commemorate the twentieth anniversary of the Cuban troops over the CIA trained rebels. It gives a very detailed overview of the invasion of the Bay of Pigs. The American attack turned into a fiasco. The space used for the display of personal items of those who died there is painfully impressive.

454 MUSEO CAMILO CIENFUEGOS

Yaguajay

The crucial Battle of Yaguajay was won by Camilo Cienfuegos in 1958 because Battista's troops ran out of gunpowder. The fall of the city was a great boost for Che Guevara's troops, as they made their way to Santa Clara. This excellent museum gives a good overview of the battle. After his victory, Camilo Cienfuegos was always referred to as 'the hero of Jaguajay'.

455 MUSEO PRESIDIO MODELO

Nueva Gerona
Isla de la Juventud

This panoptical prison was built under Machado. The five dome-shaped prison buildings are surrounded by mountains, midway between the village and the sea. Fidel and Raul Castro as well as other survivors of the failed attack on Moncada barracks were imprisoned here. After Castro's triumph in 1959, this became a prison for political prisoners. In 1967, the government ordered this prison to be closed.

PASEO DE MARTÍ

45 RANDOM FACTS AND URBAN DETAILS

The 5 most
IMPORTANT DATES

---

456 **16 NOVEMBER 1519**
BIRTH OF HAVANA

Havana was founded in 1519 by Diego Velázquez from Spain. At the time Havana was not yet the capital of Cuba. This role was reserved for Baracoa. Havana had to wait until 1607 to officially become the capital of Cuba.

457 **10 OCTOBER 1868**
FREEDOM OF SLAVES

The Ten Years' War was part of Cuba's fight for independence from Spain. The uprising was led by Cuban-born planters and other wealthy natives. On 10 October 1868, sugar mill owner Carlos Manuel de Céspedes and his followers proclaimed independence, the beginning of the conflict. Céspedes freed his own slaves as an example for everyone else. Nowadays 10 October is commemorated as a national holiday in Cuba and known as 'El grito de Yara', the place where the revolt started.

458 1 JANUARY 1959
TRIUMPH OF THE CUBAN
REVOLUTION

The Cuban revolution originated in an armed revolt led by Fidel Castro, which culminated on 1 January 1959 in the end of the dictatorship of Fulgencio Batista and the settlement of the communist movement.

459 17 APRIL 1961
THE BAY OF PIGS INVASION

Failed invasion on 17 April 1961 by more than 1400 Cuban exiles who opposed Fidel Castro at the Bahia de Cochinos or Playa Giron. The invasion was financed and directed by the U.S. Government. Launched from Guatemala, the invading force was defeated within three days by the Cuban Revolutionary Armed Forces. This failed operation strengthened the position of Castro's leadership as well as his ties with the Soviet Union.

460 1991
COLLAPSE OF THE SOVIET
UNION AND THE SPECIAL
PERIOD

The Special Period was a euphemism for an extended period of economic crisis due to the collapse of the Soviet Union. Shortages of hydrocarbon energy, resources in the form of gasoline, diesel and other petroleum derivatives occurred upon the implosion of economic agreements between the petroleum-rich Soviet-Union and Cuba. This period radically transformed Cuban society and the economy.

5 of the best
RADIO STATIONS

461 RADIO REBELDE
96,7 FM
Calle 23 no 258
entre L y M
Vedado ③
+53 7838 4365
www.radiorebelde.cu

Cubans listen a lot to the radio. Whether you understand the language or not, do turn on the radio. It is an important information channel as the Internet is only just becoming more widespread. Radio Rebelde was founded by Ernesto Che Guevara in the Sierra Maestra on 24 February 1958. The station broadcasted first-hand reports about the battles against the Batista army including operations carried out by the urban underground movement.

462 RADIO PROGRESO
90,3 FM
Infanta no 105
esq Calle 25
Centro Habana ②

Founded in 1929, they broadcast musical and cultural programs. Their most popular program is 'Alegrías de sobremesa'. This humoristic-musical program was created by the writer Alberto Luberta. The program promotes Cuban artists and is founded on a comic screenplay, 'La onda de la alegría'. Live performances are organized in Studio 1, which holds an audience of 300 people. A really unforgettable experience.

463 RADIO TAÍNO
93,3 FM
Calle 23 entre L y M
Vedado ③
+53 7838 4459
www.radiotaino.cu

This radio also broadcasts 24 hours a day. Their recreational and cultural profile targets a general audience. Listen from 5 pm till 7 pm to 'El Exitazo', true to their slogan 'lo que mas suena, lo que mas se escucha'.

464 RADIO RELOJ
101,5 FM
www.radioreloj.icrt.cu

If you need to know the time, there's always Radio Reloj (reloj means watch). They inform you about the exact time by the minute. This means the news also has to be read in one minute.

465 HABANA RADIO
106,9 FM
Plaza San Francisco Asís
Habana Vieja ①
www.habanaradio.cu

Habana Radio broadcasts from the Office of the Historian of the city. They also produce music CDs and multimedia. All proceeds from their activities are invested in the maintenance and renovation of the historic city center.

462 RADIO PROGRESO

5 ways for
CHANGING MONEY
as quickly as possible

---

466 BANCO METROPOLITANO

O'Reilly no 266
esq Compostela
Habana Vieja ①
+53 7862 7310

There are two currencies: Pesos Convertibles or CUC, the currency that will cover most of your expenses and the Pesos Cubanos, CUP or moneda nacional. You can use Pesos Cubanos to pay fruit on the market for example. Both currencies are accepted in a lot of places but there are still places where only one or the other is the rule. If you need Pesos Cubanos, you will first have to change some money into CUC, after which your CUCs can be changed into Pesos Cubunos. The Peso Cubano notes feature Cuba's national heroes. 25 Pesos Cubanos are the equivalent of 1 Peso Convertible.

467 CADECA VEDADO

Calle 23 entre K y L
Vedado ③

Cadeca has a faster service and more interesting opening hours comparing to most of the bank offices. Except from the office of Banco Metropolitano mentioned here above that is open until 7 pm, also on Saturday. Standing in line is part of your trip. Never mind, mostly the line moves quickly.

468 CADECA HABANA VIEJA

Obispo entre Aguacate
y Compostela
Habana Vieja ①

While standing in line there will always be someone asking you to change your money on the street. But you already know of course that it's better and safer to change your money inside.

469 ATM

Calle 23 y J
Vedado ③

There is a growing number of ATMs in Cuba. Remember, however, they only work with your VISA credit card. Your credit card will be debited in USD. Also check which notes the ATMs dispense. Some ATMs only dispense 5-CUC notes. When you need a large amount, it's like winning the lottery. Other ATMs can be found in Calle 23 entre N y O, Vedado, in Calle 26 esq a 37, Nuevo Vedado, Calle Calzada entre G y H.

470 HOTEL HABANA LIBRE

Calle 23 y L
Vedado ③

You can change money in several hotels. Habana Libre is one of them. Hotel Nacional (not in the central hall, there only guests can change money, you have to go downstairs), Hotel Sevilla and Parque Central are other options.

The 5 best places to
CONNECT
TO THE WORLD

---

471 CALLE 23

"Voy pa' La Rampa a conectarme" is a common phrase nowadays to say you're going to spend some time online in Calle 23. A large part of this street is a Wi-Fi zone. This means you can connect to the Wi-Fi by logging in to Nauta with a 2-CUC card you can buy in the *telepuntos* of Etecsa. If you didn't manage to buy one, there are always vendors on the street, hawking cards for 3 CUC.

472 SAN RAFAEL

Another Wi-Fi zone where you can connect to the Internet with a Nauta card. Sit down on the benches for a while. Going online becomes a collective activity. Don't forget to take your headphones with you if you want to make a call.

473 HOTEL PARQUE CENTRAL

Neptuno entre Prado y
Zulueta
Habana Vieja ①
+53 7860 6627

There's a Wi-Fi bar in the new wing of the Hotel Parque Central. You'll pay 6 CUC for one hour of internet and a complimentary drink. Don't forget to ask for your drink because they will forget it.

474 HOTEL NACIONAL

Calle 21 y O
Vedado ③
+53 7836 3564

Here you cannot use the Nauta cards to connect to the Hotel Nacional-network. You pay 10 CUC for a login and password here for one hour online. The Centro de Negocios also has a few computers you can use.

475 HOTEL EL BOSQUE

Calle 28A
entre 49A y 49C
Kohly

The best Internet connection we found. The connection is fast, even in your hotel room, meaning it's not restricted to the lobby area. Here a Nauta card will set you back 4 CUC. So buy them at Etecsa instead. You'll find many people in the small park in front of the hotel, who spend a good part of the evening connecting to the world.

5 good-to-know
DOUBLE STREET NAMES

476 **CALLE 23**
   LA RAMPA

Calle 23 is a central busy street in Vedado district. It begins at the sea and ends at the river Almendares. Its first five streets, from Malecón to L street are known as la Rampa, literally the Ramp, because they are on a slope.

477 **CALLE G**
   AVENIDA DE
   LOS PRESIDENTES

This avenue takes its name from the monuments that line the wide promenade, honouring some of Cuba's former presidents as well as other important figures, among them, the Cubans Calixto García and José Miguel Gómez, the Chilean Salvador Allende, the Venezuelan Simón Bolívar, and so on. Most locals simply call it Calle G, following the alphabetic order of the street names in Vedado.

478 TENIENTE REY
BRASIL

Calle Teniente Rey is a street in busy Habana Vieja. The street owes its name to Félix del Rey, the lieutenant of the island's governor in 1781. Under the Republic, the name was changed into Calle Brasil. Both names are used. So if you're looking for Calle Brasil on a map, sometimes you'll only find Calle Teniente Rey or vice versa. This can be confusing.

479 PASEO DEL PRADO
PASEO DE MARTÍ

Construction began in 1772 under Don Felipe Fonsdeviela y Ondeano, Governor of Cuba, who is considered Havana's first town planner. In 1884 it was remodelled, gaining prominence with improvements. In the late twenties, as part of the expansion led by the French landscape architect Jean Claude Nicolas Forestier, the bronze lions, lamp posts and marble benches that are still here today were added. The street was officially renamed Paseo de Martí in 1904. Most locals simply call it 'El Prado'.

480 AVENIDA MACEO
MALECÓN

The official street name of the Malecón is Avenida Maceo. The Malecón was primarily built to protect Havana from the water and the so-called Nortes but in reality the street ended up being used for night-time promenades by Habaneros, by lovers and fishermen.

The 5 best
BUDGET TIPS

---

481 STAY AT A CASA PARTICULAR

Book your stay in a casa particular or bed and breakfast. This is cheaper than a hotel and it's easier to get to know Cubans. Breakfast is always good in *casas particulares*, starting with a large plate of fresh fruit containing guava, papaya, pineapple and small bananas. In 90% of the casas you can also order lunch or dinner at an extra cost. They always prepare excellent *comida criolla*.

482 BOOK YOUR RENTAL CAR IN ADVANCE

By booking your car in advance you will not only save money but also time and stress. A good option is *www.cubacation.net*. In the high season renting a car when you get there can be very, very difficult.

483 USE MONEDA NACIONAL

Buy all you can at local markets using moneda nacional. The same goes for transport, use buses and almendróns. The 3-Peso note has an image of Che, you'll find Camillo Cienfuegos on the 20-Peso note, Carlos Manuel de Céspedes on the 100-Peso note and so on. 25 Pesos Cubanos are the equivalent of 1 Peso Convertible.

484 IF YOU STAY AT A HOTEL, MAKE YOUR RESERVATION BEFORE LEAVING

If you prefer a hotel, you can also save money by booking from home. The prices are better and you will have already paid (less money to take with you as not every hotel accepts credit cards). You will receive a voucher that you have to print out at home. The system works very well as long as you have your voucher.

485 BUY NAUTA CARDS FOR THE INTERNET

At the *telepuntos* de Etecsa you can buy prepaid cards to connect to the Wi-Fi with your phone. This will cost you 2 CUC for one hour. Once online you can also call your phone using the IMO app. This app works best in Cuba, so download it if you think you'll need it. To make domestic phone calls in Cuba, buy a prepaid telephone card in Pesos Cubanos to use in public phones.

5

DICHOS CUBANOS

you will hear over and over again

---

486 LO QUE SE SABE NO SE PREGUNTA

Don't ask what you already know. An important phrase in Santeria. Several Cuban artists have used this theme in their songs: *El artista soy yo* by Maikel Blaco y su salsa mayor, *Lo que se sabe no se pregunta* by Angelito y su banda, *Quien no ha dicho una mentira* by Los Van Van.

487 NO ES FACÍL PERO TAMPOCO DIFÍCIL

It isn't easy, but it isn't difficult either. You will hear this sentence regularly, it expresses a certain optimism and resourcefulness when faced with difficulty. Saying it isn't difficult is the equivalent of saying it isn't impossible so while it isn't easy we'll try it anyway. This is exactly what the Cuban comic Pánfilo told Obama during his phone call to the White House. Watch and enjoy a good laugh at *www.whitehouse.gov/blog/2016/03/19/president-obama-gets-phone-call-pánfilo*.

488 LA VIDA TE DA SORPRESAS, SORPRESAS TE DA LA VIDA

Life gives you surprises. A famous lyric from the song *Pedro Navaja* by Rubén Blades, also mentioned in *Que cosas tiene la vida* by Pupy y Los que Son, Son and many others.

489 SI NO TIENE DE CONGO, TIENE DE CARABALÍ

The Yorùba are the largest ethnic group in Cuba, the most secretive African culture in Cuba is Congo. There's a Cuban saying that says that every Cuban has to do with one of both cultures, Congo or Carabalí. Carabalí refers to Calabar, in the south of Nigeria. More generally, this proverb refers to the fact that we all have black blood flowing in our veins no matter how white our skin is. We're a great mix.

490 COMO NO SOY BONITA, TE LO AGRADEZCO MAS

A sentence from a well-known Cuban fairy-tale called *La cucarachita Martina y el ratoncito Perez*. One of the animals passing by the house of cucarachita, Martina the cockroach, tells her how beautiful she is and she answers with this popular saying which means, "since it's not true that I'm beautiful, I'm all the more grateful".

The 5 most interesting
VERSES *and* **QUOTES**
by Cuban authors

---

491 JOSÉ MARTÍ

Cuba's foremost national hero, a writer and leader who was martyred in battle.

Like stones rolling down hills, fair ideas reach their objectives despite all obstacles and barriers. It may be possible to speed or hinder them, but impossible to stop them.

492 NICOLÁS GUILLÉN

Cuban poet of social protest and leader of the Afro-Cuban movement in the late twenties and thirties. He is best remembered as the national poet of Cuba.

We've got Chinese, white, black and mixed; but remember that our colors are cheap, for after many years of contracts and tricks nobody's purity runs very deep.

493 GUILLERMO CABRERA INFANTE

Critic, journalist and novelist.
Best known for his *Tres tigres tristes*.

*What I do believe is that there is always a
relationship between writing and reading,
a constant interplay between the writer on
the one hand and the reader on the other.*

494 DULCE MARÍA LOYNAZ
VERSES 1920-1938

Dulce María Loynaz is the 'Grande dame'
of Cuban poetry. In 1987 she won Cuba's
National Literature Prize and gave a
reading at the José Martí national library
on her eighty-fifth birthday. *Garden*, still
unpublished in Cuba at the time, was
adapted by Cuba's National Ballet starring
Loynaz's friend, Alicia Alonso in the
leading role.

*I broke every road I walked.
Then I stood alone
and faced the night*

495 REINALDO ARENAS

Cuban poet and novelist. His autobio-
graphy *Before the night falls* was made into
a film by Julian Schnabel in which Javier
Bardem starred as Arenas.

*To discover a city is in itself a unique event, but
when we have the privilege of sharing it with
friends most dear to us, it becomes a once-in-a-
lifetime experience.*

The 5 must-knows to
UNDERSTAND CUBA

---

496 LIBRETA

The ration card was introduced shortly after the Cuban Revolution. The American embargo, which was designed to instigate rebellion by causing hunger, failed largely because the *libreta* was introduced. Every month, people are entitled to a number of basic products such as rice and beans. Cubans pay about 20 Pesos Cubanos for the reserved share, which they buy in the bodega.

497 JUGAR DOMINO

People are really passionate about dominos in Cuba. You will always run into people playing dominos in street corners. The games can be very animated and players will drink their fair share of rum while playing.

498 YUMA

Yuma is a word Cubans often use to refer to Americans and other foreigners. The word *gringo* is not used in Cuba. This is the Mexican word for Americans. The word *yuma* is rarely used in an offensive sense.

499 JINETERISMO

Traditionally a jinetero or jinetera will try to receive money in various ways so they can improve their living conditions. Although you can easily recognize them, always be careful in your analysis. Cubans are all very outgoing and it would be sad not to enjoy this aspect of Cuban society out of fear of jineterismo.

500 NOVELA

When you walk through the streets in the evening, you will end up hearing the same sound emanate from almost all the houses, in stereo. Everyone watches Brazilian or Mexican telenovelas, regardless of their age, or whether they are men or women. Then, after watching the episode, everyone analyses the actions of the characters in great detail.

496 LIBRETA-BODEGA

INDEX

COLOPHON

EDITING *and* **COMPOSING** — Magalie Raman

GRAPHIC DESIGN — Joke Gossé and Tinne Luyten

PHOTOGRAPHY — Roel Hendrickx (www.roelh.zenfolio.com)
— p. 133: Magalie Raman

COVER IMAGE — Ildefonsa Someillan, San Lázaro no 1016
entre Espada y Hospital, Centro Habana (secret 501)

The addresses in this book have been selected after thorough independent research by the author, in collaboration with Luster Publishers. The selection is solely based on personal evaluation of the business by the author. Nothing in this book was published in exchange for payment or benefits of any kind.

D/2016/12.005/19
ISBN 978 94 6058 1892
NUR 506

© 2016, Luster, Antwerp
www.lusterweb.com
info@lusterweb.com

Printed in Italy by Printer Trento.